GOOD
AS
GOLD

GOOD AS GOLD

The Story
of the
Carlson Companies

by Curtis L. Carlson

Published by Carlson Companies, Inc.
Carlson Parkway
P.O. Box 59159
Minneapolis, MN 55459-8202

Cover and book design by Black Dog Graphics

Printed in the United States of America

Library of Congress Catalog Card Number 94-94352

ISBN 0-9641890-0-3

To my father and mother
Charles and Leatha Carlson
my faithful and loyal wife Arleen
my daughters, Marilyn Nelson
and Barbara Gage, and their families
plus the thousands of Gold Bond
and Carlson Companies employees.
over these past fifty-six
wonderful, glorious and
Productive years.

Curtis L. Carlson

CONTENTS

ACKNOWLEDGEMENTS

THIS BOOK has depended, from beginning to end, on the effort and assistance of several persons, not all of whom are mentioned in its pages. I am grateful to Doris Campbell, my executive assistant, who helped keep the project on track; to my old friends and colleagues H.W. ("Harry") Greenough, retired vice chairman of the Carlson Marketing Group, and John Heim, retired vice president for legal affairs and special assistant to the president, for their recollections and counsel; to Carlson mainstays Dee Kemnitz, currently vice president for employee benefits, and Ann Richardson, vice president for planning and design with the Carlson Hospitality Group and vice president, Carlson Companies, who read and advised me on the manuscript; to businessman, civic leader, and author *extraordinaire* Harvey Mackay, for his encouragement and advice; to journalist Marshall Smith, who provided much of the early research; to writer and editor William Swanson, who shaped the manuscript into its current form and then directed its ultimate publication; to Robert Kemmet and his colleagues at Photos, Inc., in Minneapolis, who have taken such good care of our visual memories over the years.

My special thanks go to Thomas D. Jardine, vice president-public relations/public affairs, and Tona C. Erickson, public relations coordinator and executive secretary, who have guided this project from inception to publication. It is mainly on account of their patient hard work that you now hold this book in your hands.

Finally, I am indebted to my wife Arleen, my daughters Marilyn Nelson and Barbara Gage, and their families. Without them the life and work described on the following pages would be unimaginable.

—C.L.C.

FOREWORD

SOMEONE ASKED CURT CARLSON how he felt about the five-day work week. He said it was a marvelous idea. . . for his competitors. Curt has always felt that Monday through Friday were the days for staying even with the pack. The weekend, when the other guys take time off, that's the time to get ahead of the competition.

As Curt puts it, "You don't say 'Whoa' in a horse race."

A few years ago Curt went to Oklahoma City to be honored by a foundation that operates a museum dedicated to the free-enterprise system. Each year the foundation holds a black-tie dinner honoring three outstanding achievers. Curt was one of those being honored that night, and I was there to give the keynote address.

When Curt arrived for the cocktail party before the dinner, I introduced him to one of his fellow honorees—naturally, a corporate giant like himself. A few minutes earlier I'd learned that the fellow had flown into town in his personal 747.

The two men had no more gotten past the *nicetameetchas* when suddenly Curt startled the group by saying to the other man, "Say, did you know your company spends $2.4 million a year on corporate travel? Unfortunately, we don't see any of that. If you let us have a crack at it, we'd do a damn fine job. You see, when I knew I was going to get a chance to meet you, just before I flew down here I looked up those numbers."

At the time, I felt as if I'd hit a three-hundred-foot air pocket, but it was just a smooth ride at cruising altitude for

Curt. And you can be sure he got a crack at the other honoree's business. That's why Curt is running a multibillion-dollar company, and that explains why he's the consummate salesman. "Bass are where you find them," Curt likes to say. "And when you find them, you cast your line."

CURT'S BUSINESS ACUMEN is so widely known and celebrated that stories of this kind are common, but too little has been written about Curt's sense of humor. About the time Curt snared his Oklahoma City award, America was holding a national election and I was hosting an election eve party. Since it was November, the Minnesota weather gods decided to attend, too, and we were socked with a nasty ice storm.

Curt arrived with Arleen in his "love boat," a new Lincoln big enough to sink the iceberg that sank the *Titanic*. As usual, Dan Rather declared an electoral winner before the tube had even warmed up. Then it was time to go. That is, until the car-parker informed Curt that his car had slid off our ice-coated driveway, careened through a stand of trees, and wound up a total wreck on the frozen lake below. Did I mention the *Titanic*? Curt didn't turn a hair. He arranged a ride with a neighbor, said goodnight, and without a backward glance at his stricken behemoth rode calmly off in the storm.

The next day our doorbell rang and a messenger delivered an invoice for "One car, $37,432.22," accompanied by a note that read:

Dear Harvey,

No problem taking 2% off the invoice if paid within 30 days. Nice party.

Best wishes,

Curt

It was a lot funnier than it would have been if we both didn't have insurance.

I'VE KNOWN and experienced Curt Carlson for more than twenty-five years. I can describe his success, but I'm not sure I can explain it. Curt Carlson is a combination of so many remarkable qualities that I prefer to enjoy him rather than analyze him.

Curt has been more than a friend to me and to his community. He's been the person to go to when things needed to get done. . . the top of every "A" list in town. . . whether it's the Minneapolis Convention Center, the Hubert H. Humphrey Metrodome, the Minnesota Orchestra, or the crown jewel of his generous nature, the establishment of the Curtis L. Carlson School of Management at the University of Minnesota. Not only did Curt make the largest single donation ever made to a public university, $25 million, he led the campaign to raise an additional $365 million and personally gave millions more, once again delivering more than he promised.

Curt Carlson is a remarkable man in many ways, but unlike most remarkable men, he is not a mysterious one. Ask him what he thinks, and he will tell you. If he doesn't know the answer, he'll tell you that, too, and then he'll proceed to get the answer and let you know what it is.

Curt would be the first to say that while he has been almost fanatical about setting goals and working hard and living all the other homely virtues learned at Horatio Alger's knee, that was not what has made him what he is. Credit must go first to Curt's customers, his colleagues and employees, and, most important of all, his family. Curt isn't about numbers; he's about people. He understands people. And they understand him. It sounds simple, but, of course, it isn't. Curt Carlson connects with people.

Curt's father became an entrepreneur, a successful one, after working a dozen years for someone else. Curt's mother also worked outside the home, rather unusual for a woman at that time, and, even more unusual, she, too, ran her own business. Thus Curt's entrepreneurial instincts run deep, and his belief in the American dream, like his parents', is limitless. That belief was his greatest inheritance and to this day stokes his legendary drive.

IT'S BEEN MORE THAN 50 YEARS since Curt wrote his first monetary goal on a slip of paper and put it in his wallet, but that doesn't mean the horse race is over. From my perspective, the pace, if anything, seems to be picking up.

There is the challenge of ratcheting up the Carlson Companies' revenues another billion or two and expanding the scope of knowledge at the Carlson School of Management. There is the pleasure of enjoying the love and companionship of friends and business associates, Arleen, their children and grandchildren.

For Curt Carlson the joy and excitement of the race has always been in the running itself. There will never be a finish line.

And although we know we'll never catch him, we also know that sharing the race with Curt is the adventure of a lifetime.

—*Harvey B. Mackay*
Chairman and Chief Executive Officer
Mackay Envelope Corporation
Minneapolis

INTRODUCTION

THE BOOK you are about to read covers my life and work from the second decade of this century to the present time. Some might say they are one and the same thing—my life and my work—and to a significant degree they'd be right. To talk about one without talking about the other would be like talking about, well, Procter without Gamble.

But while describing the birth, growth, and diversification of what we now know as Carlson Companies, Inc., I have tried to make clear that my life has been enriched by many things in addition to my business: my family and friends, the Twin Cities community, the University of Minnesota, and Hennepin Avenue United Methodist Church foremost among them. Without the love, guidance, and encouragement of family and friends, without the support and nourishment of my home town, without the education and supply of talent provided by the U of M, without the spiritual invigoration offered by my church, what I've managed to accomplish in my business would have been impossible. They are an integral part of the Carlson Companies story.

While I have had the help of family, friends, colleagues, and consultants, this is essentially *my* telling of that story. It reflects my perspective on events, based on my recollections, impressions, and interpretations. I don't claim total recall for myself or total comprehensiveness for the book. There are, I'm sure, names and events that I should have included but have not. These omissions are the result of either a fallible memory or the constraints of time and space. I'm sorry if my lapses and the lapses of the book cause hurt feelings, because its intent, from the beginning, has been to celebrate the great things we many members of the Carlson family have accomplished together.

This book, you should know, was begun more than 15 years ago as a corporate history. We hired a freelance journalist, Marshall Smith, to go through company archives and to interview both past and present managers and employees—especially those who were active in the formative years of Gold Bond, the original Carlson company. Smith did an admirable job. The resulting manuscript, however, seemed dated almost before it was finished, mainly because we were growing so fast and in so many directions at the time. It seemed as though we were trying to take a snapshot in the middle of a hurricane. Finished but incomplete, the manuscript was never published.

Several years later, as the business began evolving into more or less its current shape, I was persuaded by advisors both within and outside the company to tell the story of the Carlson Companies myself, from my personal, admittedly subjective, point of view. I was, after all, the only person who has been on the scene literally from day one and who remains on the scene to this day. Encouraged by my staff and assisted by freelance writer and editor William Swanson, I decided to turn our corporate history into a corporate autobiography.

Getting started on the new manuscript, I discovered, was easy. It was an adventure, bittersweet at times, sifting through memories from my childhood, from my high school and college years, from those early, incredibly exciting—also incredibly anxious and uncertain—days of the business. I especially enjoyed reliving the glory days of the trading-stamp phenomenon, when stamps helped revolutionize retailing in this country and abroad and eventually provided the solid foundation on which today's diversified businesses have been built.

Deciding where and when to stop, it turned out, was the hard part. At one point we decided, for instance, that our fiftieth year in business would be an appropriate conclusion—only to see the need for an additional chapter and for some revision of a couple of earlier chapters. The problem was similar to the one we faced with the original history. To an even greater extent than the Carlson Companies of the '70s and '80s, the Carlson Companies of the early '90s was a multifaceted and dynamic enterprise. While it had a definite beginning, it was very much a continuing saga. Why we ended its story where we ended it was one of several arbitrary decisions that have gone into the production of this book.

At any rate, my basic objectives for this project are the same as they were at the beginning. First, I want to pass along a record of the first fifty-plus years of this company. Second, I want to acknowledge the contributions of many of the persons who have been instrumental in the company's success. Third, and perhaps most important of all, I wish to share with you—and especially with the young entrepreneurs among you—the joy of building a business, the thrill of closing a big sale, the satisfaction of working hard and, after many setbacks and detours, breaking through and earning the prize.

If some of that excitement becomes real for you, then I'll consider this book a success.

Growing Up

FIFTY-PLUS years ago, when I started out in business, I had no specific ambition to be a millionaire, to own a yacht and an airplane, or to be on anyone's list of the rich and famous.

I wanted to make money, sure. I wanted to provide a comfortable life for myself and my family. Having grown up in a conservative, middle-class home and having come of age during the Great Depression, I wanted some financial security.

But fifty years ago, when I got started, what I wanted most was, plain and simply, to get ahead, to make something of myself—*to be somebody*. Success, as I envisioned it then, did not carry a specific dollar value or prestige quotient. Success, I thought, would be its own reward.

As God and my family know, I was willing to work for it. I was willing to put in long hours, long days, long weeks. I was willing—and, strange as this may sound today, even eager—to sacrifice more immediate satisfactions and rewards to the longer-range goal of success.

In that sense, I was no different from many, maybe even most of the young people of my generation. Fifty years ago, the business of America was, as the man said, business, and to be a businessman was a noble, patriotic calling. To be a successful businessman was to create jobs and expand opportunity and make the most of the advantages you were blessed with as an American. I'm neither a genius nor a wizard. I've never thought I was given any special aptitude for numbers or market strategy or any of the other skills that set some business leaders apart from their colleagues. I have been blessed, however, with a firm and loving upbringing, good health, and a wonderful family. And I have always been willing to work.

There's not much mystery about the source of the work ethic in my family. My father, Charles Carlson, arrived in America at the age of three; he and his family had come here from the Småland region of Sweden, where the Carlsons had farmed the hard, rocky soil for generations. Once in the United States, my father's family made their way to Chisago County in east-central Minnesota, where they bought land and began farming again. My mother, Leatha, was born in America, on a farm near Downing, Wisconsin, of a Swedish mother and a Danish father, and at an early age went to work as a maid in the home of the local Methodist pastor.

Eventually my parents came down to Minneapolis, where they were married in 1905. My father drove a sprinkler wagon for the city and spent a year studying at a local business school. Later he went to work for a big Minneapolis grocery wholesaler. He was a salesman, calling on small neighborhood grocers, and he worked awfully hard at it. I didn't realize it when I was little, but he commonly put in about fourteen hours a day. Many times we didn't have our dinner until after eight o'clock at night. We were waiting for him to come home from work.

My father worked for that wholesaler for twelve or thirteen years. Then he went into business for himself. He bought a triangle of land at the intersection of 44th Street and France Avenue, in the southwestern corner of Minneapolis, and opened his own grocery store. There was a house on the property, and that's where we lived. It was —and still is—a very pleasant middle-class neighborhood in a lovely part of the city.

But my parents didn't slow down even after my father was established on his own. As a matter of fact, my father built up a terrific grocery business on that corner. He was an excellent salesman, and he was pretty shrewd with numbers. In those days, grocers delivered. Before long, my father had three trucks going from morning till night, delivering groceries all around that part of the city and the next-door suburb of Edina.

My mother was busy, too. She was raising the five of us kids. She was washing the clothes and cooking the meals and taking care of the family finances. Then, if that wasn't enough, she and my aunt opened a little bakery on the corner. That bakery, by the way, was strictly the women's business; my father had nothing to do with it. I was still very young at the time, and don't remember much except crawling under the counter of that bakery and falling fast asleep!

My father all the while was also quietly dabbling in real estate. Buying and selling parcels of land is not the kind of activity a kid is likely to pay much attention to, but I do remember one evening when Dad's real estate business kept interfering with our dinner.

I was, again, quite young at the time, yet I remember that evening as though it were yesterday. We were sitting around the dinner table when the telephone rang. My father got up and talked on the phone for a while. Then I heard him say, "No, it would have to be more than that."

When he returned to the table he said to my mother, "My gosh, we've been offered $19,500 for this triangle."

We were sitting there thinking how much money $19,500 was when the telephone rang again. This time when he returned to the table, my father said, "Gosh, another guy just offered me $21,500 for the property! I wonder what's going on."

Well, what was going on was this: Standard Oil wanted the property for a filling station. My father eventually sold the triangle to Standard, and for many years there was a filling station behind the grocery store. I can't say how much my father ended up making on the deal, though I'm certain it was plenty for those days. At any rate, it was enough to give my father the capital he needed to really develop his business.

For all my parents' industriousness and accomplishments, however, we never considered ourselves even remotely well-to-do. Everybody, including us kids, always worked as though the wolf were at the door. My father, it seemed, was always on the job. Sundays we went to nearby Lake Harriet Methodist Church, and then my father would sit in his big chair and read the funny papers to us. But every other day and evening you could be sure he was tending to his business.

My mother, for her part, was a very frugal woman. She made sure, as the family's comptroller, that we never wanted for the basics. At the same time she was never one to splurge. She believed that you made do with what you had—or you simply did without. I can remember her saying with some pride: "We will never have a lot of fancy clothes in this family, but we will always have food on the table."

I think everybody was surprised when my father, who passed away in 1968, left behind an estate of $300,000.

M Y PARENTS always wanted us kids to be hardworking and independent.

Like most immigrants and children of immigrants in those days, they ardently believed in the importance of education and the necessity to assimilate and be "good Americans." Both my father and mother spoke fluent Swedish, but neither one gave us kids the slightest encouragement to learn their native language. The Carlsons were Americans now, not Swedes. I think they were afraid that we would grow up speaking English with an accent.

Looking back, I can't say my childhood was any different from the childhood of thousands of other kids growing up in Minneapolis at the time. I was born July 9, 1914, the third child in a family that would eventually comprise four boys and a girl. Like most of the other kids in the neighborhood, I attended the nearby public schools, skated, swam, and played sandlot baseball and football.

I suppose I was a shy kid—not exactly timid or withdrawn, but independent, a kid who liked to keep his own counsel. One thing I remember for sure: I was not allowed to accept candy or gum or anything else from the other kids. I was expected, as were my brothers and sister, to get the things we wanted for ourselves.

That meant that as soon as it was practical, we were supposed to go out and earn our own spending money. My parents would tell us, "If you want something, fine. Go out and earn the money to buy it." They pointed out that there were all kinds of ways for kids to earn money. Even in the depths of the Depression, there was more work than a young fellow could handle. There still is. I can't tell you how much it bothers me to see page after page of want ads in the paper, knowing that there are all those jobs and yet millions of people out of work.

I couldn't wait to get to work. I got my first real job —delivering the old *Minneapolis Journal*—when I was ten. I started out as a substitute for another carrier. When he couldn't enroll any more new customers, I told him that I knew who wasn't taking the paper and that I'd try to sign them up. In fact, I asked him, if I signed up a half-dozen new customers, could I take the whole route, and he said fine. Well, I went out and enrolled the six new customers, and from that point on the route was mine.

I maintained that paper route all through junior high school, high school, and well into my college years. During all that time I always worked like mad to add customers. I kept enrolling new customers until I was finally down to only two houses on the whole route—but, to save my soul, I couldn't land those two. I recall how those two hold-outs infuriated me. They infuriated my mother, too, and for a long while she and I refused to speak to either one of them.

It's funny, though, the things that happen. One of those two hold-outs was a family by the name of Zimmerman. For several years I can remember walking past their house and getting angry because I couldn't toss a *Journal* on their stoop. Then one day I got a call from Mrs. Zimmerman. She asked me to come over, which I did as soon as I'd finished my route. I was thinking, of course, that I was finally going to get the Zimmermans' business. As it happened, Mrs. Zimmerman had something else in mind. "Curtis," she said, "as you know, we're very active in the Democratic Party. Well, my husband has been given the privilege of naming a boy to the Naval Academy. We were wondering if you would like to go to Annapolis when you finish high school."

Needless to say, I was surprised and puzzled. I told her I would think about their generous offer and let them know the next day. It was interesting to think about, but, frankly, the thought of going into the Navy instead of going into business left me cold. I went back the next day and told them no thank you. Already, at the age of sixteen or seventeen, I wanted to be a businessman more than anything else in the world. The Zimmermans were disappointed. But, despite the fact that I never did get their newspaper order, we were very good friends after that.

My first paper route, back in 1924, paid me $15 a month.

Well, it didn't take a genius to figure out that if one route earned a fellow $15 a month, three would bring in $45. I soon asked for a second route, promising the manager I'd keep adding new customers, and eventually I took on a third. I organized my brothers and sister as helpers, and together we made that business really go. At one point, I also sold papers at a newsstand downtown.

It was tough work, as any of you who have ever had a paper route know well, but, so help me, I loved almost every minute of it. Some days I was positively ecstatic.

I remember when the Minneapolis Auditorium first opened in 1927. The *Journal* was giving special coverage to the national Rotarian convention that was being held there, and someone had the bright idea of selling special one-week subscriptions to the delegates. That way, while the delegates were in Minneapolis for their big conclave, their families back home could keep abreast of the activities.

I went down to the Auditorium with a fistful of subscription blanks, not sure what kind of reception I was going to get. What I discovered were several lines, each one about fifty to seventy-five people long, with everybody waiting to register for the convention. I started at one end of one line and delivered an impromptu pitch.

"We'll send the paper right to your home," I told the first man in line. "We'll tell your family all about the festivities here in Minneapolis."

The man said it sounded like a good idea and asked how much. I said, "Only a buck," and he filled out the form. Then the next fellow said, "Here, give that to me," and *he* filled out the form. Before I knew it, almost everybody in all those lines had signed up for the special one-week subscription.

I was about thirteen years old at the time, and in one fell swoop I had earned myself $300! I couldn't believe it—and

I couldn't have been prouder if the figure had been $5,000! My parents, of course, thought the whole adventure was simply stupendous.

Besides the money and praise from my parents, there was a lesson for me as well. The experience taught me that there is always a chance to succeed in a big way, if you can only find the right opportunity.

THERE WERE OTHER JOBS, TOO, when I was a kid. There were lemonade stands to operate, lawns to mow, sidewalks to shovel, and work around my father's store.

In the summer and on spring and fall Saturdays I also did a lot of caddying. (Sundays were probably the best days for caddies, but Sundays in the Carlson household were always reserved for family and church.) One of my brothers first took me out to Interlachen Country Club in Edina when I was about nine. That first summer the going rate for caddies was fifty cents for eighteen holes. The following summer the club raised the rate to seventy-five cents for one bag and a dollar for two. In those days, that was nothing to sneeze at.

Still, it was hard work for a kid and often made for a long, wearying day. There was never any letting up. I remember one Saturday when I had the audacity to fall asleep while waiting for the 5:45 a.m. streetcar that would take me out to the club. I had caddied all day the day before, and I was just plain worn out. But, suddenly, there was my mother out at the streetcar stop, shaking me by the arm.

"And *what* do you think you're doing?" she wondered out loud. A moment later I was wide awake and aboard the streetcar, en route to the club.

Later I became an assistant locker boy at Interlachen. I

kept the place swept up and shined shoes for $50 a month. The full-fledged locker boy kept all the tips in addition to his salary. That arrangement didn't seem exactly fair at the time, but the situation didn't bother me. Fifty bucks a month wasn't bad money in those days, either.

And I must say that while I didn't really envy all those wealthy golfers I saw out there, I did like the idea of the life they were living. At that time I thought the sweetest existence in the world must begin when they'd come in off the eighteenth green, enjoy a nice leisurely shower, and then sit there relaxing with a cold drink and their pals on the veranda before going home. That must surely be the life!

But of all the jobs I had when I was very young, the most important were the paper routes. A paper route taught a kid some very important lessons. The company gave you those papers to deliver; then you would collect the money from your customers, and at the end of the month you would pay your bill from the company. What was left over after you paid that bill was yours. Thus you learned, among other valuable truths, the most basic fact of business life: that what you took in had to be greater than what you paid out.

You also learned the value of goods and services. You learned to look at sporting equipment and ice cream sundaes and even haircuts in terms of how much work it required to pay for them. A lot of kids nowadays, I'm afraid, don't know the value of the things they buy, because they don't have to work for the money they need to buy them. When all you have to do is ask for it, everything is a bargain.

To tell the truth, though, I never thought much about those early jobs as teaching me lessons that would stand me in good stead later. As far as I was concerned, they were simply the reason that I was the only fellow among my pals who ever had any money.

School Days

EDUCATION, as I said, was very important to my parents. Like many other members of their generation and background, they were convinced that education—along with hard work—was the ticket to success in America. I'm afraid, though, that I may not have taken my schooling quite as seriously as they did. I was too busy working and having a good time.

I attended West High School in south Minneapolis. Like a lot of the landmarks of my past, that handsome institution is gone now, the victim of progress and the wrecking ball; a condominium stands in its place. In my day, West High was a wonderful place. I was part of a large and very enthusiastic group of kids—the class of 1932—and, boy, I'll tell you, I had a ball!

Despite my parents' feelings, I never studied very seriously. As a matter of fact, I can't remember ever doing any homework. Though I liked sports, I was not one of the school jocks. But I was carrying all those paper routes, and I never missed a dance. I was also president of the school's Hi-Y chapter.

During summer vacations I worked. I remember one day, while making the rounds in search of a good summer job, I paid a visit to a particular employment agency downtown. This was during the early years of the Depression, and twenty-five percent of the working-age population was unemployed. At the employment agency I was told they weren't accepting anyone who hadn't finished high school. I was simply out of luck, they informed me.

Leaving the agency, I happened to start chatting with another young fellow in the elevator. He was probably a year or two older than I was, and the agency had given him some encouragement. In fact, he said, the agency had given him not one but *two* job possibilities. One was a clerk's position at the Grain Exchange; the other involved what amounted to a bellhop's job at Farmers & Mechanics Savings Bank. I asked the fellow which position he was going to try to land, and he said the one at the Grain Exchange. I wished him luck—and headed directly to the bank.

That other fellow must have taken the job at the Grain Exchange because he never showed up at the bank. The people at the bank, for their part, never asked if the employment agency had sent me. When I presented myself and inquired about the job, they gave it to me on the spot.

In those days, before computers, the bank's tellers would ring a bell when they needed information about a customer's account. A bellhop would run to the files, dig out the requested document, and bring it to the teller. It was a tiresome job, but it paid well—about $50 a month—and I held onto it, along with my paper routes, when school started again in the fall. I suppose I find that rather odd in retrospect. But I had started to save for a blue Chevy convertible, and I decided to stay out of school for a year so I could work for it. Amazingly enough, I was able to negotiate a deal with the school that allowed me, despite the year off, to earn enough credits to graduate with my class. Even more amazingly, my parents went along with the plan.

They must have been persuaded—perhaps overwhelmed is the better word—by my determination to get what I wanted.

THERE WAS NEVER ANY DOUBT, however, that I would go from high school to college. College, among us Carlson kids, was simply a fact of life. I don't think it ever occurred to us *not* to go to college. It was something that was expected, no questions asked.

That is not to say, though, that the Carlson kids sailed blithely away to a higher education on the waves of their parents' savings. No, sir! My mother and father never charged me room and board while I attended the University of Minnesota, but I paid every penny of my tuition. I also paid for my books and clothes. It was nip and tuck, I can tell you, but that was what was expected of us. If we wanted something badly enough, we could simply go out and work for it.

I did not have a specific career plan in mind when I started at the university. I once saw a paper my son-in-law, Dr. Glen Nelson, had written when he was in the fifth grade; he had decided way back then that he wanted to be a physician. All I knew at the time I went off to college was that I wanted to go into business. I took some constitutional law and a few other pre-law courses to keep my options open—and because my mother had always liked the idea of my becoming a lawyer. But I majored in economics and began piling up credits in business administration because I knew that business in some way, shape, or form was my calling.

I had a terrific time at the University of Minnesota, which I believe to be one of the great institutions of higher learning in the world. It is now, and it was then. But I really had to hustle to make ends meet while I went there. Unlike my experience in high school, where I was the one guy who always seemed to have some money, within the circle I was part of at the university, I was one of the "poor" kids. I couldn't even afford to live in the house of the fraternity of which I was president! But that's the way it was. I did the best I could with the cash I had.

After the first year or two of college, I finally gave up the paper routes that I had run since I was ten. Though I had the routes well organized and had several other kids working for me by that time, the little business wasn't bringing in enough money to justify the time and attention that went into it.

I did all sorts of other things to make money instead. Summers, for instance, I worked for my dad, who at that time owned a soft-drink distributorship. I drove a truck and hauled cases of soda pop from the warehouse to grocery stores, restaurants, and bars all over Minneapolis. Saturdays I worked all day and then into the evening until nine or ten o'clock. It was hard work and long hours, but the pay was pretty decent for its day.

When university classes started again in September, I had to come up with another, less time-consuming enterprise. I was often carrying as many as seventeen or eighteen credits a quarter and was very active in my fraternity, Sigma Phi Epsilon. Besides, I still liked to dance. To help make ends meet, I developed a little advertising business in my free time. What I'd do is have some attractive bulletin boards made up and post those boards in all the fraternity and sorority houses around campus. Then I'd sell advertising space on those boards to local restaurateurs and merchants. It was a simple idea—so simple I wondered why no one had thought of it before I did—and, better still, it worked.

That's the way it went during my college years. I'd do a little of this and a little of that—and I'd be very, very careful about how I spent a buck. My education, you see, was not confined to the classroom.

TODAY, ALMOST SIXTY YEARS after I graduated from the University of Minnesota, I look back on those times with great warmth and fondness.

Though by my senior year I was eager to get out of school and get on with a career, I truly loved the learning process. I loved listening to my professors formulate their hypothetical business problems—then dreaming and scheming and trying to figure out a way to resolve those problems and maximize a hypothetical profit. I loved reading the case studies in the textbooks and putting myself in the shoes of "real" managers and executives.

I took great pleasure, too, in the social life that revolved around my fraternity. I made many close friendships there that have passed the test of time. That fraternity activity, by the way, was as instructive as it was fun. It taught me how to deal with my peers, how to initiate and develop close, working relationships. To this day I look favorably on any job candidate who has been an officer of a fraternity, sorority, or other such social organization. To me, that kind of achievement shows that the person has a pleasing, persuasive way of relating to other people—which is, of course, a critical attribute in business. It is an absolutely essential attribute in sales.

Finally, it was at the university that I met the blonde young woman who would eventually become my wife. I first saw Arleen Martin in a political science class. She was wearing such a huge pair of glasses that I couldn't help but laugh. When she asked me what I was laughing at, I told her that those were the biggest glasses I had ever seen on a girl. Then she took them off, and I thought she was very pretty. I walked her to her next class, and we struck up a beautiful relationship. By the time I was ready to graduate, I was also having thoughts of marriage.

As I said before, though, it's funny the way some things in your life turn out. I worked like hell to finish up my senior year at the university. I took eighteen or nineteen credits per quarter that year and pulled down all A's and B's—mostly A's. Those were not, mind you, the grades I unfailingly received during the entire four years of my university career. But by my senior year I was in a hurry to get out of there, so I really bore down hard.

I did so well that year, in fact, that I received an invitation to take part in Harvard University's master of business administration program on a scholarship. I looked at that invitation and showed it to my parents, and we all sort of wondered what it meant. I did know one thing right away. I didn't have the slightest interest in going on to graduate school—even at such a prestigious place as Harvard. I wanted to get on with my life. I wanted to make some real money. I wanted to be somebody.

Not long ago I heard one of my daughters telling somebody that her dad was offered a scholarship to Harvard, where people were dying to go, dying to be accepted, and yet her dad didn't do a darn thing about that offer. My daughter may have thought I had merely been indifferent. The truth is, however, I didn't understand how valuable an MBA—not to mention a *Harvard* MBA—could have been to me at that time. Nowadays all the bright young executives seem to have MBAs; maybe eighty or eighty-five percent of the young people coming into Carlson Companies looking for jobs boast those advanced degrees. But in those days, when I was coming out of school, an MBA simply wasn't perceived to be a very big deal. The important thing was a basic bachelor's degree and the prospect of a decent job.

I've been asked, of course, how things might have turned

out if I had accepted that invitation and gone on to Harvard. Who knows? Perhaps I would have taken that MBA and jumped on some large corporation's management track and jockeyed my way toward a big corner office on the twentieth floor. Perhaps instead of eventually setting out on my own, I would have grown fat and happy working for somebody else. In retrospect I thank the good Lord for sparing me that good fortune.

I've always believed that I was blessed with a lucky star. If I could only tell you how many times, during the development of this company, I did not get my way when I wanted something—when I wanted, let's say, to acquire another company—and it turned out to our considerable advantage that I didn't. Well, that's the way I look back at that Harvard invitation. Thanks to my lucky star I was too naive to know what an MBA could do for me—too naive to know where and with what result it might have taken me.

With that MBA I may never have become my own boss, which, I was soon to discover, had been my ambition from the beginning.

Getting Started

WHEN I GRADUATED from the university with my bachelor's degree in 1937, America was still in the grip of the Depression. Despite the continuing problems, however, there was beginning to be a sense of improvement across the land, and there were jobs available to college-trained eager beavers just hitting the market. Big companies from all around the country, as a matter of fact, were beginning to recruit hot prospects right off the campus.

I was offered a sales position with the Equitable Life Insurance Company. At that time Equitable was guaranteeing a recruit $15 a week for the first year, after which he'd be on his own. That amounted to $60 month, which was hardly a king's ransom, but those were still depressed times and $60 a month wasn't chicken feed, either. Then I was offered $90 a month by Procter & Gamble. Shortly after that, Carnation came in with what at that time seemed a lordly figure indeed—$120 a month. Carnation, with headquarters in California, was at that time the largest producer of canned condensed milk in the world. It was a big, profitable company, and it was initiating an exclusive executive-training group of which, if I accepted its offer, I would presumably be a part. Needless to say, I was seriously tempted and gave the offer a lot of hard thought.

But then the district manager from Procter & Gamble came back at me. He wanted to know why I hadn't given him a definite response to P & G's offer. I told him frankly that I was torn between P & G and Carnation. On the one hand, I said, the P & G offer was attractive because the company would allow me to stay put in Minneapolis, where the girl I wanted to marry lived and where I wanted to work. On the other hand, Carnation was offering me a salary of $120 a month while P & G was offering only $90.

Like most of the people who worked for Procter & Gamble, that district manager was not about to take no for an answer. He went into a long, impassioned spiel about P & G's size and might, and about the tremendous career opportunities a company like that could offer a bright young fellow like me.

"Oh, and by the way," he added pointedly, "there's been a mistake. Our offer is *$110* a month."

Some mistake, I thought. But I just played dumb. "Oh, that's different," I said. And I signed on with P & G.

Looking back, I believe that this was another instance in which my lucky star was protecting me. That Carnation job would have been a good one, no question about it. I would have had to move out to the West Coast, but I believe I would have had a promising future. The problem would have been that the higher I climbed within the company's management, the harder it would have been for me to break loose, to start my own business. I might have been trapped in a pair of golden handcuffs and never have become my own boss.

I'd love to say that I had some grand and glorious career plan mapped out when I joined Procter & Gamble, but the truth is I didn't. I just wanted to remain in Minneapolis and enjoy the security of a regular income. I had not yet realized how much I wanted to start a business of my own.

In retrospect, however, I can see how enormously beneficial to my long-term future that first career step, with Procter & Gamble, turned out to be. Indeed today, with the benefit of both experience and hindsight, I would strongly urge every young man or woman with entrepreneurial stirrings to do what I did: spend some time learning from an already successful enterprise what the business world is all about.

Even if you don't know what kind of business you want to make your mark in, I'd advise you to, first, take a job with somebody big and successful, because you can bet that that somebody has a pretty good idea of what works and what doesn't. That big, successful somebody has spent years, maybe generations, developing, refining, and perfecting its techniques. That somebody doesn't by any means have all the answers—but it has more than you do, no matter how smart and well educated you are, just coming out of school. A good, healthy company that's been in business for many years can give you the best "advanced degree" available anywhere.

Going to work right out of college for somebody else will also give the eventual entrepreneur a chance to sample different career possibilities, different industries, different types of products and services. You may have grown up with a romantic notion about this industry or that—only to discover, by your own on-the-job experience, that it's not quite what you thought it would be. That's one hell of an important lesson, and the sooner it's learned, the better.

The flip side of that, of course, is discovering an occupation or industry that you'd never really thought much about. Having tried it, you've discovered that it precisely suits your abilities and ambitions. And you've made that discovery without having invested a huge amount of your own or someone else's money. To the contrary. You've learned while you've earned!

If, when you get out of school, you're absolutely sure about what you want to do with the rest of your life, a couple of years with a big, established company will at the very least teach you the discipline of the real world. The experience will teach you that, unlike what you may have been able to get away with in college, you cannot let a situation slide unattended and then save your skin with an all-night cram session. It will teach you to appreciate the skills and opinions of other people, to be attentive to details, and to be constantly alert to both danger and opportunity. It will help you understand the importance of a solid organization.

This is the same basic counsel, by the way, that I give my own grandchildren, some of whom would like to come and work in this company. I tell them, "Fine, we'd love to have you—but first you must go to work for someone else for two or three years. When you've learned something about the business world, when you've proved that you can move ahead on your own, come to us. Then we'll find a place for you." The point is, that early experience is crucial.

If you've got an entrepreneurial itch, you're nothing if not impatient. You can't wait to get started, to get out there on your own. Believe me, I understand. I know exactly how you feel! But I guarantee you that every little bit of on-the-job education and experience you can get while learning the ropes at that established company will pay huge dividends when you're ready to start your own.

WHEN I WAS FRESH OUT OF SCHOOL, I thought I knew a thing or two about the wide, wild world of business. I had a university degree in economics, after all. I had several years of hustling up my own tuition and spending money. I had a handful of attractive job offers to show for my study and preparation. Then Procter & Gamble taught me what the business world was really all about!

My job, at that fiercely negotiated salary of $110 a month, consisted of selling Procter & Gamble soap and grocery products to retail outlets in south Minneapolis. On the face of it, that sounds easy enough. Thanks to those long summer days working for my father, I was familiar with the territory and with many of the storekeepers along the route. I'd grown up in the grocery business and understood at least the basics of the trade. Besides all that, I believed I had the invaluable gift of gab. I suspected that perhaps I was a natural-born salesman. What, then, could be so tough about selling a little Oxydol, Ivory, and Crisco?

Well, for one thing, I discovered that selling Oxydol and Crisco was not quite the same as selling subscriptions to the *Minneapolis Journal.* When you were hustling newspapers, your basic operating principle was pretty simple: the harder you worked, the more newspapers you sold. Selling P & G products was something else again. Despite the intensive training and instruction the company had provided me, I discovered that I couldn't sell a damn thing. I worked like mad for the first four weeks, and yet, for the life of me, I couldn't make a sale!

I remember saying to Arleen, "I don't know why I didn't take that job with Carnation. All the grocers hate P & G— and hate their salesmen to boot."

Allowing for a little youthful exaggeration, there was nonetheless some truth to my complaint. Then as now, Procter & Gamble was a hardball player. P & G went directly to the consumer—in those days the housewife—with all the persuasive strength of its radio and newspaper advertising, and if the consumer couldn't find her Oxydol at one store, she simply went across the street to another. P & G, in other words, had the individual neighborhood grocer very firmly in its grip.

Operating with that kind of strength in the market, P & G salesmen were trained to come on with the aggressiveness and tenacity of pit bulls. We were conditioned to engage in some real bare-knuckles selling. The operating philosophy was captured by the phrase "aggressive exploitation." I can remember my district manager saying that if a P & G salesman wasn't thrown out of at least one grocery store a week, he wasn't selling hard enough.

That district manager was exaggerating a little himself, of course. But there was no denying that we were conditioned to be hard chargers. And for a sound enough competitive reason. Nice guys, I was beginning to realize, didn't necessarily make the most effective soap salesmen. You simply had to be persistent, had to keep coming back at that merchant, had to make sure your Camay and Ivory—not the other guy's Palmolive or Lux—dominated the merchant's precious shelf space.

When you sold for Procter & Gamble, you learned to keep meticulous records. Chances are, the merchant you were calling on didn't keep very good records himself. So when you kept track of each case of Oxydol he bought from you, you were doing him a favor. He may not have been crazy about you, but he did learn to trust your numbers. In the process you learned to be thorough and to leave nothing to chance. You even made a note about his taste in music (Mozart, say, or Glenn Miller?), about whether he liked to fish (he does, for walleye, but never seems to find the time). You didn't spend too many minutes in idle chitchat with the fellow, but you made a genuine effort to know him and understand his particular circumstances.

You also learned, when you worked for P & G, that you weren't selling soap and shortening so much as you were selling solutions to the merchant's problems. His biggest problem was keeping his store full of customers. The solution we offered was a shelf full of popular, high-quality products backed up by heavy-duty advertising and promotion, at a cost that would allow him a decent profit.

I started at eight o'clock in the morning and generally made about fifteen calls a day, five days a week. (Saturdays were the busiest days of the merchant's week; they were far too busy to allow him to "waste" time with a salesman.) Once in a while you could get by with making only thirteen calls a day, but never as few as twelve. If you made only twelve calls a day, you can be sure that you would hear about it from your manager.

I'd hit a store with my sample case in hand. The storekeeper and I would chat for a couple of minutes, then I'd check his inventory and tell him about this or that big promotion coming up, this or that special on Ivory. I learned never to tell the fellow more than three things at a time. More than three things and he'd forget them all. Maybe he would write them all down, but then he would inevitably put that slip of paper somewhere and lose it. Three things he would remember; three things he would keep in his head.

Another little trick you performed involved the ordinary pencil. When you were ready to take the merchant's order, you asked to borrow his pencil. Then, when you asked him to sign the order, you handed him his own pencil. That way you didn't come across so pushy. You weren't pulling out your own pencil and making a big show of the sale—you were simply giving him back his own.

The pencil routine was subtle, but effective. And by no means the only little trick in our kits.

PERHAPS THE SINGLE most important lesson I learned during my eighteen months selling for Procter & Gamble, however, involved the critical need to innovate, to find the ways and means to effect a breakthrough. At the age of twenty-three, I sold more soap than any other Procter & Gamble salesman west of the Mississippi River. That was not because I was smarter or more aggressive than my P & G brethren; it was because I discovered a way to break new ground in my territory.

In the late 1930s, drugstores were, to all intents and purposes, the supermarkets of their day. They were generally run by college graduates who employed a reasonably sophisticated approach to selling. What's more, they offered their customers a fairly wide range of merchandise and often generated a lot of traffic. At that time, they were selling our bath soap, though in only small, really negligible quantities.

One day I suggested to one of the larger druggists in south Minneapolis that instead of buying only a dozen bars of our soap at a time, he buy the soap in carload lots. I told him how little I could sell it to him for in that quantity, and he, being a real live wire always receptive to something new, took me up on the offer. He bought soap from me in carload lots and sold it cheap as a heavily promoted loss leader—and, by golly, he set the local drugstore business on fire. Other large drugstores on my route quickly followed suit, and suddenly I was moving an incredible amount of soap. I continued to sell to the grocers, of course, but it was the large, progressive druggists of south Minneapolis that really put me ahead of the pack.

It struck me that the situation hadn't been so terribly different from the time I sold all those newspaper subscriptions at the Rotary convention. In both instances, a breakthrough was effected by means of doing something that hadn't been done before—something novel, something untried. And, in both cases, the breakthrough resulted in a killing, albeit on somewhat different scales. An essential lesson I'd first been exposed to at the age of thirteen had been reinforced—driven home—when I was twenty-three.

What with bonuses on top of my regular salary, I was beginning to make some real money. But, money aside, I can't tell you how much *fun* I was beginning to have! Some people might say: "What could be duller than making fifteen calls a day, selling the same thing to the same people, day in and day out?" But those people don't understand the thrill of the sales game, of rising up and meeting the challenge, of competing against all the other hotshots in the field.

I loved scanning those rankings of the sales force that came out from company headquarters and seeing my name moving up that list two or three places at a time. It's funny, thinking about all the merchandise I earned through incentive programs at P & G—vacuum cleaners, household appliances, that sort of thing. In that sense, selling Oxydol and Crisco didn't seem so different from selling the *Minneapolis Journal.* Instead of being awarded a flashlight for my effort, I was now awarded a lamp!

For coming in first in my territory my rookie season, I earned a gold wristwatch and a bonus of $330. The money, of course, was appreciated, but it was the watch that by far meant the most to me. It was the watch, also, that taught me something about the value of prizes as awards in incentive programs. Because long after the bonus money was spent and forgotten, that watch would signify my accomplishment. That watch would be an ever-present reminder of the great things a fellow could achieve with some hard work, a lucky star, and a little innovation.

I worked for Procter & Gamble for only a year-and-a-half, but the lessons I learned from that relentlessly aggressive, highly disciplined company would stay with me for a lifetime.

And to this day, when I go to the drugstore, I buy only Procter & Gamble toothpaste and soap.

CHAPTER FOUR

The Birth of Gold Bond

IN THE SUNDAY FUNNIES my father used to read to us as kids, whenever one of the characters got a bright idea, a light bulb went on over that character's head. In my case, I have to admit, there wasn't any light bulb suddenly blinking on above me. It was more like a gradual dawning of awareness that eventually illuminated some very interesting possibilities.

The trading stamp was not my idea at all. In the late 1930s, when Arleen and I happened upon stamps at the old Leader Department Store in downtown Minneapolis, the idea of giving coupons or stamps with retail purchases was almost a half-century old. The trading stamp had been used for the first time way back in 1895, at Schuster's Department Store in Milwaukee. When I first encountered the idea, however, trading stamps were redeemable only for cash, were available primarily in department stores, and, all in all, were not creating a great deal of excitement.

I had never heard of the things before that day at Leader, when the saleslady gave Arleen some Security Red Stamps with her purchase. When I asked the clerk about them, she said, "Don't you save our stamps?" Then she handed us a little booklet and told us: "Put the stamps in here. When you fill up the book, we'll give you $2 cash."

I was working for Procter & Gamble at the time, selling

large enough quantities of soap, shortening, and detergent to earn myself plenty of prizes and bonuses. I was learning a great deal about the sales game and having a good time to boot, yet I couldn't help but think of the possibilities that lay beyond P & G. Thinking about that book of trading stamps we'd been given while shopping, I wondered: What if that concept—giving trading stamps as a shopping incentive—was applied by the merchants I was calling on?

The question intrigued me. A large department store, I reasoned, could offer its own exclusive lines of merchandise for a competitive advantage. A little corner grocery store, on the other hand, was selling pretty much what its competitors were selling—the same brands of soap and cereal, the same assortment of fruits and vegetables, the same selection of dairy products and canned goods. There was virtually nothing, except the difference of a few cents on this or that item, that set one of the little guys apart from the others. What would happen, I wondered, if a grocer gave out stamps with every sale?

As far as I knew, the hypothesis was untested. There simply didn't seem to be a precedent of grocers giving trading stamps. If someone was going to try it, I figured it was going to have to be me. And the more I thought about trying it, the more excited I became.

I wasn't unhappy selling for Procter & Gamble, mind you. I wasn't crazy either, so I did not, as sometimes happens in popular accounts of entrepreneurs, leap out of one career and into another. It is often said that an entrepreneur takes risks. That's true. But I believe that an entrepreneur will go to almost any length to *minimize* the risk before leaping the gap between what he knows and what he doesn't. In any case, the risk of such a leap, for a twenty-three-year-old kid scarcely out of college, was simply too great. For one thing, I knew I would soon have a wife to support—Arleen and I were planning to get married—and I knew that we wanted to start a family. For another, I was not sure that trading stamps would work the way I suspected they might. At least I was not sure enough to burn my bridges behind me.

So I continued to work for Procter & Gamble while starting my little stamp company on the side. Monday through Friday I sold Oxydol and Crisco; on weekday evenings and on Saturdays I struggled to get my own business on its feet.

I learned that Saturdays were tough days on which to sell—but so were Mondays, Tuesdays, Wednesdays, Thursdays, and Fridays. I also learned something that I've since taken great pains to tell my people and would urgently point out to anybody who wants to be an entrepreneur. You work five days a week to stay even with the other guy. You work the sixth day to get ahead.

NOWADAYS A YOUNG PERSON embarking on a new venture would probably have steeped himself in entrepreneurial theory at the university, would have read a couple dozen books on starting one's own business, and would have talked to a legion of seasoned entrepreneurs who had already gone out and done what he was dreaming of doing. All of which would be a whole lot better than the way I went about it back in 1938. But I had little choice: the theory and the books and the entrepreneurial mentors were simply not available to me when I needed them.

There were no local stamp companies to provide me with on-the-job training, either. The "giant" of the business, S & H Green Stamps, and the other major established firm, Eagle Stamps, were not yet presences in Minnesota. For that matter, the stamp business as a whole accounted for only about $15 million a year in those days, which means the stamp companies weren't exactly dominant anywhere. And, as I said, nobody, to my knowledge, was doing anything, anywhere, with stamps in the retail food business.

Besides, when a fellow is in his early twenties, he tends to be pretty cocky. He has a few more years before he starts to get humble. I just thought I would figure things out for myself as they happened.

I decided, early on, to call my fledgling operation the Gold Bond Stamp Company. The decision, though, had nothing to do with any sort of formal market research. I had been told, in an advertising course at the university, that there were two basic approaches to selecting a brand or trade name. If you had a lot of money to spend on advertising, you were advised to select something unusual and distinctive—"Lux," for example—and make it familiar through constant repetition in the newspapers and on the radio. If you didn't have a lot of money to spend on advertising, you'd be better off with something more immediately familiar, something with positive connotations. Since I was in the latter category, I chose "Gold" for value and "Bond" for safety. The name "Gold Bond," I felt, had the advantage of being short, easy to remember, and absolutely *shining* with positive connotation.

When I needed a contract for potential clients, I didn't go to a lawyer. (I didn't *have* a lawyer.) I paid a secretary at the Leader Department Store five bucks to show me the store's contract with the Security Red Stamp Company. Then I simply copied that contract and substituted "Gold Bond" for "Security Red" in the text.

Acquiring the capital I needed to get my company rolling was a little more difficult. I figured, for instance, I needed two hundred pads of stamps to get started. (A pad comprised fifty sheets with one hundred stamps per sheet.) I had some bonus money from P & G, but that was not quite enough. And because I had not yet established a credit rating, the printer insisted on his money in advance. Well, I was living in a $55-a-month apartment at the time, so I went to my landlord and asked if he would let me pay that $55 at the end of the month instead of at the beginning. I explained that I was starting my own business and was in urgent need of cash. The man was very kind. He said, "If that will help you get going, pay me at the end of the month. Call it my contribution to your venture."

That kind of encouragement was rare. In 1938 most people simply did not know what trading stamps were all about; they didn't understand how they worked and couldn't appreciate their potential. When people thought about going into business for themselves, they usually thought about making or selling something tangible. They wondered how in the world anybody could make a buck selling something like stamps. Furthermore, the notion, in those depressed days of the late 1930s, of striking out on your own with an untested "product," was, to a lot of folks, too foolhardy to think twice about.

I remember, several months after I started the company, going to the bank where I had my savings account and asking for a loan. I had put together an association of stamp-giving merchants at a busy south Minneapolis intersection and needed $900 to print new savers' books and promotional handbills. The banker, however, was not impressed with my grand plans.

"Curt," he said, "why a bright young man like you would want to quit a big, established company like Procter & Gamble is beyond my comprehension. You'd have a good job there for the rest of your life, and I'll be darned if I'm going to encourage you to leave it. The quicker you decide to stay where you are, the better off you and your family are going to be." Needless to say, he didn't give me the loan.

On the other hand, though my wife, who was looking forward to starting a family, was not wildly enthusiastic about my leaving the security of a regular income, she trusted my judgment. Her father, Charles Martin, who ran his own clothing-manufacturing business and could appreciate my itch to go out on my own, was downright excited about my venture. As for my own parents—well, I don't recall their saying too much on the subject one way or the other. If my parents had a strong opinion either pro or con, they never told me. Long before that time I think they knew that I would go out and do what I wanted to do in any case.

And, of course, they were right.

I'T'S PROBABLY IMPOSSIBLE for me to convey the excitement I felt when I landed my first account. I was still working full time for Procter & Gamble, but my confidence in the trading stamp idea was growing by the day. The original glimmer had become a glow, and the glow was getting brighter and brighter. One night it was assisted by a flashlight.

That first account had not come easy. I knew the grocery business, and I knew that south Minneapolis territory. I knew that those Southside grocers all had the same problem—keeping their stores full of shoppers. On the other side of the counter, those grocers knew and trusted me. They knew me as the Procter & Gamble man, and, if I wasn't exactly beloved of each and every one of them, I was generally respected and therefore given a fair opportunity to make a pitch on behalf of Gold Bond Stamps.

I had learned the rudiments of the sales game with P & G. I had learned how to deal with rejection. I had learned to be persistent, to keep coming back, to keep the heat on the buyer. Now I insisted, among other things, that Gold Bond Stamps would hook the grocer's customers the way an occasional special on Crisco would never hook them, and that once hooked, the customers would keep coming back for more. I told them that as long as one box of Wheaties tasted just like every other box of Wheaties, there was no better way for an individual grocer to capture and sustain a competitive advantage than by using my stamps.

Nevertheless, it was a damned tough sell. The grocers I called on were no more familiar with the idea of trading stamps than the bankers who turned down my requests for loans. Those grocers were not, as a rule, the most innovative marketers in the world. Most of them, as far as that goes, were simply too preoccupied with the day-to-day pressures of survival to stand back and coolly assess their marketing techniques. We were still in the squeeze of the Great Depression, after all, and the notion of turning two percent of their gross over to an unproven incentive program no doubt seemed crazy—if not downright criminal—to a lot of them.

Anfin Odland was as skeptical as the others. But in March 1938, Odland, who ran a little grocery on Twelfth Avenue South, was eventually persuaded to try my new program. In exchange for his initial $14.50 order, I gave him the exclusive right to redeem Gold Bond Stamps within twenty-five square blocks of his store. With that modest arrangement the Gold Bond Stamp Company was off and running!

The night before Odland's "grand opening"—the official introduction of Gold Bond Stamps—I could hardly contain my anticipation. I took Arleen and drove over to the store, where we stood on the sidewalk and peered in through the darkened window. I shined my flashlight through the window on all the balloons and banners and signs proclaiming the availability of Gold Bond Stamps, and I shivered with excitement. My excitement, I should point out, was not bound by Twelfth Avenue, by Odland's twenty-five-block trading area, or even by the limits of the city's South Side. My excitement was bound only by the limits of the theory of replication—whatever those limits might be. I had learned the truth of the theory of replication years earlier, when I was selling and delivering the *Minneapolis Journal*. Simply stated, the theory held that if one paper route earns X amount, three paper routes will earn three times X—or more.

That magical March night in front of Odland's store I had that theory on my mind when I said to Arleen: "Now I know I can sell the idea. If it works here, there are *thousands* of stores all over America that will buy it!"

ANFIN ODLAND'S GROCERY STORE was a telescope that allowed me to see the blazing possibilities of the future. And the introduction of Gold Bond Stamps in that modest Southside establishment gave me a rush of exhilaration like no other thrill in my life.

After that first account, the others began coming in their turn. I was not exactly overwhelmed by the demand for stamps, but there was no longer any significant doubt that I was selling something that people wanted. I had the confidence born of that initial breakthrough, not to mention the first actual evidence that my stamps could work the way I believed they would—that they could dramatically increase a grocery store's business. Several of my accounts were already registering a fifteen to twenty percent increase in sales. It was time I began to give serious thought to burning the bridge to P & G.

I had, by that time, already taken steps toward my

entrepreneurial independence. On June 8, 1938, I'd registered the Gold Bond Stamp Company with the state of Minnesota. I had established a small office—a mail drop, really—in the Plymouth Building in downtown Minneapolis. I was paying another businessman's receptionist $5 a month to answer the Gold Bond telephone. I soon began employing the first of two daytime managers to run the business for me when I was out hustling Crisco and Oxydol. My little stamp company, in other words, had just about everything it needed except a full-time boss at the top.

Contrary to what some people may think, there was no dissatisfaction with Procter & Gamble. I was by that time making $150 a month, plus the bonuses, and having a high old time watching my name rise to the top of the monthly sales lists. I had, in everyone's opinion, a terrific future with the company. On the other hand, I was beginning to sell my stamp plan, and I was increasingly convinced that I was on to something substantial. Meanwhile, the two managers I hired to help build the business didn't seem to be able to handle the job. I just don't think either one of them ever quite understood the product he was supposed to be selling. At any rate, they both seemed content to sit around and wait for the phone to ring instead of making every hour count out on the pavement. I finally decided that if I was going to do the job right, I was going to have to do it myself. All it required, I figured, was the guts to abandon a promising career.

After eighteen months of regular employment, I said goodbye to P & G. There were no hard feelings on either side. In fact, contrary to their policy, my boss said that if the stamp business ever flopped, I'd be welcome to come back. Not that I expected it to flop, but I appreciated the man's gesture. My enthusiasm for stamps was by now unquenchable, but I was not totally free of anxiety about making the leap. His offer helped allay whatever fear I might have had.

I have heard the phenomenon of going out on one's own compared to jumping from an airplane. Well, I've had the good sense never to jump from an airplane, so I can't vouch for the accuracy of that comparison, but I can tell you that when I leapt free of Procter & Gamble I felt a tremendous surge of excitement. The exhilaration I felt at the freedom to work as long and hard as I wanted and to keep everything I earned by my labor is quite beyond my powers of description. Immediately and instinctively I knew that I had made the right choice.

I had never given thought or voice to the specific definition of the word "entrepreneur." But I realized, at that moment, that an entrepreneur is what I was born to be.

CHAPTER FIVE

The Early Years

I HAVE ALWAYS WORKED toward goals, be they newspaper subscription prizes or Procter & Gamble bonuses. I was brought up, as I've explained, to decide what it was I wanted and then to work until I had it.

But while I'd like to say that my initial goals for my fledgling stamp company were high, wide, and handsome, the fact is they were really quite modest—particularly by today's standards. I had no grand plan, no grandiose vision of either Curt Carlson or the Gold Bond Stamp Company five or ten years down the road.

I wanted to be in business for myself, and I wanted to be a success. In somewhat more specific terms, I remember deciding at the time that I wanted to earn $100 a week. I didn't even set myself a deadline. I simply wrote "$100 a week" on a slip of paper, put the paper in my wallet, and buckled down to work. I think I reached that goal in about a year, at which point I threw away the first slip of paper and replaced it with one that said "$200 a week." I've had slips of paper with my goals written on them tucked away in my wallet ever since. They were modest goals at the beginning, but they were always specific—goals against which I could measure my progress. Of course, my personal goals quickly became company goals: Curt Carlson and Gold Bond Stamps were more or less synonymous.

If there's a lesson in this, it's simply that success is something most often achieved incrementally, one modest step at a time. Many young entrepreneurs think big—and that's all right. But more important is to plan in detail what must be done month by month to achieve each year's objective toward realizing the Big Dream. Planning without a realistic timetable is meaningless—tragic in some cases—because impatience often gets over-eager entrepreneurs in trouble. Businesswise, they bite off far more than they can chew and then find themselves choking on their own ambition.

Eager as I was in those early days of my enterprise, I was not leaping immediately for the gold. For one thing, with little or no precedent to guide me, I had to inch my way along like an explorer of uncharted territory, making my own marks as I went. For another, I had to educate not only myself in the ways and means of saving stamps, but the public as well. For still another, I could move no faster than my limited capital would allow me.

Capital, of course, is crucial to the entrepreneur. It was then, in the early days of Gold Bond Stamps, and it is today, after more than fifty years in business. Then as now, you had to be very prudent about how you spent your capital and how you conserved it.

I've learned that a successful entrepreneur is a person who reduces his risks as much as he possibly can. That's because before he is a successful entrepreneur, he's just another little guy starting out. He can't afford to risk too much of what precious capital he's managed to beg, borrow, or steal. He has a realistic budget that he follows with care, and no more organization or infrastructure than he can absolutely afford. He sweeps out his own office, which at the beginning may be merely a desk in his basement, and perhaps he asks his wife to do his typing. He does not hire another person until he has more business than he can handle by himself.

A fellow once said to me, "Curt, how is it that you knew

all that when you were just starting out?" I laughed and said, "I didn't. In those days I didn't have enough capital to do it any other way. With the little resources I had to start with, I had no choice but to be frugal."

When I was getting started, capital was extremely difficult to come by. The country simply had not accumulated the capital it has today. There weren't the venture capitalists that there are today, and the banks were ultraconservative. You would have to collateralize everything you owned before the banks would give you any help.

Initially, in my case, there was the bonus money from P & G, a few dollars in my savings account, and the fifty-five bucks generously deferred for thirty days by my landlord. Then there were whatever deals I could cut with my suppliers. I've mentioned, for instance, the $900 I had to come up with to pay for some saver books and handbills. Well, when my banker wouldn't grant me the loan I'd asked for, I went and talked to the printer. I told him that I had already gotten the business, and that if he'd carry me until my clients paid up, he'd have both my business and my sincerest appreciation. Luckily for me, he finally agreed to my "terms." I wasn't bluffing about the business. It was there, all right. I paid the printer off quickly and had cash left over for my next campaign.

Actually, the money I had to put out for the stamps themselves was a relatively small part of my expenditures, even early in the game. The big expense came a little later, when the customers redeemed their stamps for cash. In the meantime, however, I would have collected my payment from the stores to whom I had sold the program, and that gave me the working capital to increase the business.

I charged a customer $14.50 for a pad of stamps. If that entire pad of stamps was redeemed, I would pay out a total of $10. But here there was another factor working for me. It was a fact of life that at least five percent of the stamps given out by a merchant were, for one reason or another, never turned in. There was nothing secret about the percentage of these unredeemed stamps. The Internal Revenue Service was vigilant in following that number and eventually developed a complex formula that resulted in stamp companies paying income tax on all redeemed stamps, plus seven percent more for unredeemed stamps instead of the statistically proven five percent. As a result, many stamp companies found their reserve fund inadequate to redeem all the stamps presented for redemption.

In any case, the unredeemed stamps, plus the profit over and above Gold Bond's overhead, amounted to pre-tax earnings of $1, or six percent of sales—not too unlike the earnings of most other service businesses.

WHEN I FIRST STARTED OUT, I worked out of my own apartment. Then I moved to the tiny office in the Plymouth Building in downtown Minneapolis. Finally, after I'd parted company with P & G, I set up shop in a storefront office at 106 South Eleventh Street, still within the downtown Loop. I paid $35 a month for that space, not counting heat and electricity. I divided the space into a forward area for the public, a center office for myself, and a back office for my assistant, Joe Hunt.

Joe was my first full-time employee. He was a couple of years younger than I was and had studied accounting in a Civilian Conservation Corps camp. I hired him because I needed someone to keep the books while I was out selling. As it turned out, I couldn't have found a better person for the job. The two of us worked smoothly together—he as the "inside" man and I as the "outside" man—even on Saturdays and Sunday mornings, and he stayed with me for several years. His was, of course, a critical job. A businessman can misspell a word now and then and get away with it, but he'd better be sure that his arithmetic is correct. Like my dad, I was pretty good with figures, but I no longer had the time to spend on them. I needed to be out selling. Thus I left the numbers and the order-filling to Joe.

Once I was on my own, I worked every bit as hard as I did with P & G. Harder, actually. I would go into the office every morning, because, then as now, I strongly believe that the person in charge has to be available to make the major decisions, whatever else he may have to do. But by nine o'clock I would be out on the street again, making my calls. I had no illusions about my primary responsibility as an entrepreneur. My role, first and foremost, was to sell.

The number of calls I'd make in those early years varied. On the average I'd say there would be at least five or six a day. Now that is fewer than half the number of calls I used to make for P & G, but the ones I was making now involved a different, more complicated kind of sell. With P & G, I was selling the same, familiar product every time. There was very little I had to explain. With Gold Bond Stamps, I was selling a new and unknown concept. Now *everything* had to be explained.

You could tell the grocer, for example, that you have a surefire way for him to increase his volume. But you'd also have to tell him that once he came in, it would be awfully difficult for him to pull out. It was no longer such an easy matter as telling me he didn't want my damn Crisco this week! In those days I insisted on a ninety-day contract with a customer. (Later, when we were offering gifts and we had showrooms full of inventory to worry about, the contract was lengthened to a year.) Beyond that stipulation, there was the grocer's customer to consider. Once she starts saving the stamps, I had to explain to the grocer, she's probably not going to want to quit. There will always be just one more book to fill, then one more after that. For both the grocer and the customer, it could easily become a never-ending story.

I had many ways of sweetening the appeal for the grocer. If he would sign up with Gold Bond Stamps, I would blanket the neighborhood with promotional handbills, I'd fill his windows with flashy advertising, I'd festoon his walls with banners and balloons. For many of the little guys I called on in those days, all the promotional hoopla I provided with the stamps was easily worth the $14.50 he'd pay me for his initial order.

But it was a peculiar thing. You could have a terrific salesman who would never be able to sell the idea of stamps. On the face of it, a trading stamp was nothing more than a little square piece of paper with glue on the back. Viewed another way, however, that little square of paper represented a revolutionary way of doing business. That was difficult for some fellows to understand, much less get across to potential customers.

The ultimate customer of the stamps—the individual saver—had to be educated along with the grocer. When I sold a new account, I had to hire a person to go from house to house throughout the neighborhood explaining the benefits of the little glue-backed pieces of paper the corner grocer was about to start giving them with their purchases. If I were merely to put up a sign in the grocer's window saying "We Give Gold Bond Stamps," nobody would know what all the hoopla was about.

Like most of my lessons, I learned that one the hard way, by trial and error. I didn't send anyone around the neighborhood at first, and the grocer often didn't realize the increase in business that he'd been promised. The grocer would say, "Hey, Curt, nobody knows what this stamp business is all about." Then he'd advise me: "Why don't you go on the radio or put a big ad in the paper?" Well, I could no more afford sixty seconds of radio time or a full page of newspaper space than I could afford a yacht on Lake Minnetonka. What I could afford was a guy who, for $3 a day, would canvass the neighborhood surrounding the store and spread the good news about Gold Bond Stamps.

The fellow would eventually cover about sixteen square blocks around the store that was introducing the stamps. At every house he would give the homemaker a saver's book and stamps and explain how they worked—how, say, at Henry Johnson's grocery over on 41st Street, the shopper would earn one stamp for every ten cents she spent, and how the stamps, when a certain number had been saved, could be redeemed for $3 in cash (or, a few years later, for name-brand merchandise). We always gave her twenty-five free stamps to get her started, plus a coupon for another hundred free stamps with her first order.

The door-to-door education paid off. Before long, the "We Give Gold Bond Stamps" sign was as familiar—and as self-explanatory—as virtually any advertising pitch in the participating grocery stores. And the little gold squares of paper themselves were becoming almost as familiar as the greenbacks for which they were initially redeemed.

So THERE WAS PROGRESS, to be sure, but there were always a lot of problems to solve. Maybe that's what has made my business—what makes most businesses—so interesting. No matter how much you grow, no matter how much success you achieve, there is never any end to the problems. Some business people call them "challenges" or "hurdles." Some prefer more colorful terms. By any name, they're a pain in the neck that the entrepreneur must forever reckon with. Let me give you a peculiar—and especially troublesome—example.

One of the reasons I moved into those new quarters on South Eleventh Street was the presence of a big furnace in the basement. I wasn't overly concerned about our personal comfort during the long, cold Minnesota winter; I was more concerned about burning all the Gold Bond Stamp books that were being redeemed. In the beginning I'd simply burned the used books in my fireplace at home. Then I needed something with greater capacity. The furnace at the South Eleventh Street location proved to be an excellent incinerator.

As my business increased, however, so did the sheer volume of stamp books that had to be destroyed, and before long there were far more books to be burned than even that furnace could handle. I piled books in that furnace until the grates melted down and dropped into the ashes. I replaced the grates, but by that time getting rid of the redeemed books had become an almost full-time endeavor. I had to come up with something more practical.

The paper shredders manufactured in those days were far too small and slow, so I eventually got a fellow to develop a simple machine that would punch a hole through every stamp in the redeemed books. The machine was placed in every redemption center—at that time there were three-hundred-thirty of them around the country—and it worked pretty slick. But direct mail orders eventually amounting to ten percent of our redeemed books (literally millions of dollars annually) were being stolen here and there before arriving at our warehouse. The pilfered books had not yet been punched full of holes, so they could be cashed in a second time, and there was no way to stop it. I simply had to find a method to plug the ever-growing leak.

We began hauling the books to the municipal garbage dump. The city said it was fine for us to dispose of our problem there, so we'd back our trucks up and drop the redeemed books into an enormous pit, where a steamshovel would pick up the rubbish and toss it in a huge open-top furnace. That seemed to be the perfect solution until I received a letter from the wife of a worker at the dump who had just been fired. The woman said she thought I'd like to know that some of my most enthusiastic "redeemers" were the wives of the city's sanitation workers! It seems some of those workers were grabbing the stamp books before they made it into the inferno. The thieves were stuffing the books in their pockets and God knows where else, then taking them home for their wives to cash in.

We had one hell of a problem over the course of several years. We even had instances of truck drivers tossing boxes of books to their wives—who were waiting at pre-arranged drop-off points—as they drove the redeemed books to a disposal site. That technique, in fact, became such a serious problem that our accountants finally had their own people following the trucks all the way to their destination. You would have thought we were dealing in real gold!

In later years we began using our own giant shredders in very tightly controlled surroundings, and that, at last, seemed to reduce the dimensions of the problem. I can't tell you how much we might have lost to pilferage and theft over the years. I can tell you that some years ago one of my competitors was taken to court by his creditors. The creditors complained that instead of paying off his debts, the man had gone out and bought himself a boat—a second boat, as a matter of fact, the second one being even larger than his first.

Testifying in his own defense, the man explained that he had to have a larger boat in order to stay in business. He said he was hauling weighted sacks of redeemed stamp books out to sea and dumping them in the ocean. Divers, however, had taken to following him and were going after the sacks, so he needed the larger boat to haul the stamps out past the continental shelf, where he could dispose of them beyond the reach of the underwater scavengers.

The judge said the fellow's story was preposterous. But I understood his problem perfectly and couldn't have been more sympathetic.

CHAPTER SIX

Waiting Out
the War

I CAN'T HELP BUT SMILE when I hear people talk about "overnight sensations." The truth is, most of the individuals, institutions, and corporations we like to think of as sudden successes have struggled for years before acquiring any real measure of achievement.

There are no doubt those who believe that the Gold Bond Stamp Company was an overnight sensation—that, once educated to the miraculous potential of trading stamps, a grateful merchandising public beat a path to its door on South Eleventh Street. Well, that's an awfully nice idea, but, unfortunately, it's not true. The company's actual success was anything except instantaneous. As a matter of fact, it never occurred to me that I might strike it rich in a month or two. Which was a good thing considering it took us more than fifteen years of grassroots selling before the big grocery chains became aware of our successful marketing formula.

We got off to a decent start—there's no question about that. With Joe Hunt tending to the "inside" aspect of the business, I was doing what I did best: spending long and increasingly profitable days "outside" making calls. Our educational efforts were beginning to pay off. Grocers, then druggists, then filling-station operators were getting wise to the benefits of giving stamps, just as their customers were quick to catch onto the benefits of saving them.

When one skeptical grocer wondered aloud whether Gold Bond Stamps would do everything I was telling him they would, I'd reply, "Don't take my word for it. Call any grocer that gives them and ask him what my stamps have done for *his* business." The skeptic would call, and the grocer he talked to would be more than happy to crow about his stamp-induced increase in business. As more and more merchants signed up with Gold Bond, more and more skeptics were converted into believers.

Part of my early strategy was to go after what I called "associate accounts"—handfuls of small merchants and service establishments clustered around a thriving city intersection. This was long before the coming of the huge suburban shopping malls, remember. Most people's day-to-day shopping was done in their neighborhood, on busy corners near their homes. Typically there would be a grocery, a meat market, a drugstore, a dry cleaner, maybe a little dry goods or gift shop, and a filling station. By selling to all of the merchants and tradesmen in a cluster, I would form an "association" of Gold Bond Stamp givers who'd have a potent competitive edge over other such groupings in their part of the city.

The idea of increased customer sharing became a powerful new selling tool. If the grocer gave Gold Bond Stamps, his customers would be inclined to trade at the drugstore next door if the druggist gave them, too—and vice versa. What's more, if four out of five establishments in a cluster gave stamps, customers would fill their saver books quickly and urge other merchants to give stamps also.

By the summer of 1941, three years after the company's founding, Gold Bond boasted more than two hundred accounts. We were doubling sales every year. By now we

were spreading out across the state, no longer limiting ourselves to Minneapolis and St. Paul. We were on a roll, and
we knew it!

I had hired my first full-time secretary, a nineteen-year-
old graduate of a Minneapolis business college named Alvina Lenzen, but there seemed no end to the work. Ten or
more hours a day, six and seven days a week was the rule.
Like my father before me, I was never home for supper
before seven-thirty or eight o'clock in the evening. The business was virtually all-consuming. I was eating, sleeping, and
even dreaming about Gold Bond Stamps.

I readily admit that while I was building a business for
myself, I might well have destroyed my tiny family. I would
not be either the first or the last person to sacrifice a spouse,
children, and "normal" home life on the fires of entrepreneurial ambition. Sad to say, it often happens. It is not
inevitable, but the entrepreneur and the entrepreneur's
spouse had better know what they're getting into right from
the start. They had better understand the possible risks every
bit as well as they understand the potential rewards.

Arleen and I had been married for only about three
months when I left Procter & Gamble and struck out on
my own. She was a bit apprehensive, of course, but she made
it clear that she was behind me one hundred percent in
whatever I wanted to do to earn us a good living.

Before the first of our two daughters was born, Arleen
even pitched in herself. She dutifully dressed up in a Gold
Bond drum majorette's uniform and handed out savings
books, printed instructions, and promotional brochures at
our grand openings in the larger markets. She was what you
might call a "demonstrator," putting, say, thirty free stamps
in a saver book and handing it to a curious shopper—
demonstrating how easy it was to save stamps. Even later,

after both of our daughters were born, Arleen made no complaints about the incredible amount of time and energy I was channeling into the business. She understood and accepted both my ambition and the demands of starting my own business, and for that I will be eternally grateful.

I have seen plenty of cases—here, in my own company, as well as in many other organizations—where a marriage is torn apart because there wasn't that kind of understanding and acceptance. As far as that goes, I've seen plenty of cases where a business is crippled or destroyed by domestic pressures. The truth is, an entrepreneur cannot afford to fight a rear-guard action at home while battling to establish a beachhead in the business world. It won't work, and everybody, including some innocent kids, are probably going to suffer.

My advice to the fledgling entrepreneur is this: Make sure your spouse is with you one hundred percent on your venture *before* you begin. Make sure your spouse understands that there will be long hours and countless distractions and, at least for a while, a lean family checking account to show for all the sacrifice. If your spouse can't or won't make the necessary adjustments—well, you'll simply have to ask yourself what you love most, your spouse or your business. And you're going to have to make a choice.

You may be well advised to go to work for an established corporation, and content yourself with a safer, less demanding career, where you can give more time to your family.

O F C O U R S E, N O T E V E N A L O V I N G and supportive family is going to guarantee your success. In those early years before the United States became involved in World War II, the Gold Bond Stamp Company had its fair share of downs as well as ups. Sometimes a grocer would decide he simply didn't like giving trading stamps, and, after a trial period of a few months, would pull his store out of the program. Sometimes we were the victim of our own success, having to scratch and scramble for cash to pay for all the handbills, saver books, and sundry promotional materials that became necessary when we landed a big associate account. Sometimes, like everybody else, we were swept along on the currents of larger events.

I suppose that every member of my generation remembers where he or she was when first informed of the Japanese attack on Pearl Harbor. Joe Hunt and I were standing on ladders. We were putting up our Gold Bond signs at a department store in St. Paul when we heard the shocking bulletin that December Sunday in 1941. Like everybody else, we were stunned, then angered and alarmed, then bewildered by the news. We knew that the coming of war was somehow going to affect our lives, but we didn't know in what way or to what extent. Joe and I—that is, the Gold Bond Stamp Company—would find out soon enough.

By the middle of 1942, barely six months after America entered the fight, our business had been slashed by two-thirds—from some two hundred accounts to roughly sixty—and the remaining third were shaky. The loss was the result of nothing personal, nothing we did wrong, nothing we could have planned for or worked to overcome. The dynamics of the market had suddenly and radically changed as the nation rushed off to war. In a time of shortages and rationing, who needed incentives to get shoppers into grocery stores, butcher shops, and gas stations? Who, in other words, needed trading stamps?

Furthermore, with all the bright young talent either enlisting or getting drafted, it was soon apparent to me that I wasn't going to build much of a sales force. My own thin ranks were soon to grow even thinner. Joe Hunt enlisted in the Navy, Alvina Lenzen in the women's Marines. Despite my having a wife and child, I myself was classified 1-A— ready for the draft. Eventually I closed down my home office on Eleventh Street and moved what little remained of the Gold Bond Stamp Company to a separate room in a children's ready-to-wear store that, on the side, I had started in partnership with my father-in-law.

I had learned a good lesson with Gold Bond. America is such a huge market that it takes only one idea to be successful. I quickly made the Klad-ezee children's store a model of its type and wrote a manual on how to operate a successful children's wear shop. You couldn't buy the manual at any price. You had to join my voluntary chain of franchised shops to get it. We gave this manual out free and listed the franchisee in our weekly ad in the two largest newspapers in the five-state area. Martin Bros., the manufacturer, continued its usual schedule of monthly ads in the children's wear publication. In return for an exclusive in its town, the franchisee had to carry our entire line. Having the advertised merchandise on hand when the ads ran was an elementary necessity.

The cost of setting up Klad-ezee shops in many cities was nominal. The main store in Minneapolis that I opened still ran our weekly ad. Only now our logo at the bottom had listed all the Klad-ezee franchises throughout the area. The same was true of the national ads—only now they were larger and, with the added coverage, more effective. The forty-four Klad-ezee stores eventually accounted for half of our total national sales. It was true: America is a huge market, it takes only one idea to be successful.

One day, expecting as I was a greeting from the draft board, I went over to see the Navy recruiter. I had taken part in the Reserve Officer Training Corps program at the University of Minnesota, and at that time the Navy was more or less routinely giving college graduates commissions, so I told the recruiter I wished to sign up as a lieutenant junior grade. After all, I had achieved the rank of sergeant in the R.O.T.C.

The recruiter laughed and pointed out that it was customary for young officers to begin at the ensign level.

I told him that with my business experience and so forth I probably had a little more than the average enlistee to offer the Navy, and since I was taking the trouble to volunteer. . . .

But the man was unmoved. He said that I could enlist all right—but as, and only as, a lowly ensign. There were limits, I discovered, to my personal salesmanship.

Well, I thought, maybe I could bargain for something a little better when the time came, so I went back to work and waited for the notice from my draft board. I was originally told I had about three months to get my house in order. My house, of course, was one thing; my wife and daughter would be taken care of by our respective families when I went off to war. But what about my business? I wondered. Who would take care of the Gold Bond Stamp Company while I was away?

I decided, after no small amount of worry, searching, and consideration, that the best available man for the job was a Procter & Gamble supervisor in Wisconsin named Truman Johnson. Truman was too old for the draft, yet young enough to keep the fires burning at Gold Bond. I told him, "I'll give you forty percent of the company's stock if you leave P & G and come to work for me. Whatever the company makes, you take forty percent and turn sixty percent over to my wife."

Truman, however, wanted fifty percent. I could understand his position, of course, what with P & G offering a somewhat more secure career than my skimpy little outfit offered at the time. Furthermore, I didn't think I was in any position to turn the man down. For all I knew, I was going to be drafted the following morning. I said, "O.K., Truman," and handed him fifty percent of the firm.

The war went on, but I never heard a word from my draft board. Then my second daughter was born, and I was reclassified 1-B, my name sliding lower on the list of prospective draftees. Meanwhile, by about 1944, the company's fortunes were apparently bottoming out. Things were at long last beginning to look up. We had managed to hold on to a handful of solid grocery and drugstore accounts, and now were gradually beginning to recoup some of the filling-station trade we'd lost. Interestingly, the filling-station owners discovered that they could get all the gasoline they wanted. The only catch was that they had to turn in the rationed gas stamps the government issued to every car owner. Gold Bond again provided the magic by pulling in these coupons.

As the fortunes of war turned both in Europe and in the Pacific, our business also began to improve. There was no dramatic turnaround, no breathtaking, sudden surge up and onward. We were, as I said, anything but an overnight sensation.

As far as that went, I was never even a naval ensign. When the war ended in 1945, the draft board had never called.

Breaking Through!

THE END OF THE SECOND WORLD War brought an unprecedented prosperity to America. It also brought back Gold Bond's business—slowly and in relatively small pieces at first, then with an enormous bang that signaled the beginning of an unprecedented prosperity in the trading-stamp industry.

Selling stamps was particularly tough sledding during the war, but we kept at it. Toward the end, as I said, we even began to make some progress. Truman Johnson and a new recruit, Vernon McCoy, were beginning to open new markets for us in Wisconsin, while here at home I was working hard not only to get back what we had lost, but to sow the seeds of future growth. Thinking about the millions of servicemen who would soon be returning home, starting families, and buying groceries, I accelerated my planning and began rebuilding the organization. Thus, when the war finally ended, we did not have to start over from scratch.

The immediate postwar years were even busier than I expected. Trading stamps were catching fire across America. We were not only selling them to grocery stores, filling stations, drugstores, and the other "traditional" big-city neighborhood merchants. We were breaking new ground with such unlikely-seeming accounts as small-town and rural movie theaters, feed mills, even turkey hatcheries and mortuaries!

We were also beginning to sell entire states at a time,

using aggressive district managers to open and develop the new territory. In 1946 we came up with the slogan "It Shall Be Done by '51," which reflected our absolute determination to be doing business in seven states within the next five years. We made it, too, though the seven states we ended up with by 1951 were not the seven we originally had in mind. In addition to Minnesota and Wisconsin, they included California, Nebraska, North Dakota, Iowa, and Michigan.

Most important, we were little by little perfecting the stamp concept. We were learning from our mistakes as well as from our successes—which is another way of saying we were gaining valuable experience.

I have often said that I did not build a company, I built an organization. By that I mean that I developed a group of aggressive, persistent, hard-working people who were geared to succeed and perpetuate the company's development. Some people may have described it as a perpetual-motion money-making machine, but that rings too mechanical in my ears. What we were then—what we are now—is a living, breathing, growing organism, comprised of dedicated people committed to a single goal: to forge ahead, to succeed, to grow ever bigger and better.

In those first few exciting years of postwar expansion there were plenty of good men and women from whom to choose for the organization. They were coming out of the service by the millions, able and eager young people like my brother Dean, who flew for the Navy during the war, joined us upon returning home, and soon became a district manager in Wisconsin.

I was especially interested, however, in people with backgrounds in the food and grocery trades. Just as I did coming from Procter & Gamble, they would know their way around a grocery store; they would know the lingo and the mechanics of the business. More than that, they would understand the pressures of a tremendously competitive marketplace, and the need to drive hard, to persevere, in the face of that competition. Vern McCoy, for instance, came to us from Van Camps, the big canning company. And I believe it was no accident that so many of our most successful sales people—our strongest horses—have come to Gold Bond with food-merchandising or grocery experience.

In the five or six years right after the war I moved Gold Bond headquarters from the few hundred square feet on the mezzanine of the Klad-ezee children's wear shop I owned in partnership with my father-in-law to a series of larger and larger offices. It is a testament to our speedy recovery from the wartime doldrums that we always seemed to be growing too fast for our new space to be sufficient for very long. I remember, for instance, crowding a couple dozen people into some office space designed for half that number at the North American Life & Casualty building near Loring Park, on the edge of downtown Minneapolis. Things were so tight that we literally had to turn sideways in order to pass between the desks.

We had also taken on, for the first time, an outside advertising agency—Bernie Fishbein's one-man shop—to help us polish up our promotional materials and more firmly establish a corporate identity. It was Bernie who came up with the slogan "Save Gold Bond Stamps and Suddenly It's Yours!" Bernie also developed the frugal little Scotsman we happily dubbed Sandy Saver, who quickly became the Gold Bond trademark. In one pose or another, Sandy was soon appearing on the covers of our savings books, on all our billboards, store signs, and handbills, even on the ballpoint pens, cufflinks, and tie clasps we handed out as promotions.

I won't say that the presence of the smiling, kilted Scotsman ever quite reached the enormous proportions of the Jolly Green Giant, another familiar Minnesota-based trademark, but he might have come pretty close. In any case, Sandy was a vibrant sign of those busy times and, for us, a harbinger of good—no, *great*—things to come.

A LL DURING THOSE immediate postwar years something revolutionary was happening in the grocery business. The big supermarket chains were beginning to take the place of the smaller independent stores, the traditional little mom-and-pop operations that over the preceding decades had become permanent—or so we thought—fixtures in every neighborhood of the city. The chains had been around, albeit on a modest scale, since the middle 1920s. But now, with a new kind of sophisticated consumer seeking greater selection for her grocery dollar, the chains represented the wave of the future.

In the late 1940s and first couple years of the '50s we were busy selling stamp programs to the little guys. Though their overall numbers were rapidly decreasing, there were still an awful lot of them, and more than ever they needed stamps in order to compete. Many smaller merchants, while remaining independent, were in fact becoming bigger and more aggressive, and were hungry for fresh competitive strategies and tools. Our salesmen were continually on their doorstep, and were selling them a program that worked.

We were at the same time acutely aware of the giants looming larger on the horizon every day. In the Twin Cities the largest of the grocery chains—National Tea, Red Owl, and Super Valu—were taking a heavy toll among the smaller independents. In one year more than five-hundred grocers went out of business in Minneapolis alone. It was a sad but inevitable development. The war and its dislocations had changed countless aspects of the way we lived, including the way we shopped for groceries. We had more money to spend and we wanted a greater variety of goods to spend it on. We were more mobile, what with two cars per family, and thus less confined to the immediate neighborhood. We were willing to serve ourselves, to push our own shopping carts, and we didn't need to have our order delivered. We were increasingly amenable to paying cash for our grocery purchases in exchange for buying them at generally lower prices.

From a purely business point of view, those grocery chains represented potential trading-stamp sales I wouldn't have dared imagine before the war. The hitch was, the chains hated stamps. They loathed the very idea of stamps— almost to the point of paranoia. Our salesmen dutifully and persistently called on them, but, for the first several years following the end of the war the salesmen met with absolutely no success.

Then something began happening. Those giant chains, having gobbled up much of the smaller competition, began to realize that they would have to find ways to compete among themselves. All of them were "buying in volume" and "selling for less," which was quite enough to set them apart from the old-fashioned small-time grocer. But what they needed now was something to set themselves apart from each other. Furthermore, they realized, with no small amount of distaste, that when given a choice, most shoppers preferred receiving trading stamps to a handful of extra change. Trading stamps were a tangible "thank you" for their patronage.

This is not to say that the supermarket door suddenly

swung wide open to trading stamps. The local National Tea manager said that while he was no longer opposed to stamps, he would have trouble getting approval from his corporate bosses in Chicago. Red Owl executives said they were interested, but still had several reservations. Officials at Super Valu, the most congenial of the three local chains, said they would be *more* congenial if the stamps could be redeemed for merchandise instead of cash. Once again we had to be patient and persistent, and take one step at a time.

Finally and ironically, both Red Owl and Super Valu decided—during the same week in 1952—to experiment with stamps in some of their stores. Red Owl, however, was insisting that we charge them only one percent of gross sales instead of the customary two. Super Valu, though firm in its wishes to have the stamps redeemable for premiums, was agreeable to the standard two-percent charge and willing to explore more fully the possibilities. Super Valu executives were dispatched to Texas and other parts of the country where stamps were beginning to catch on among the larger markets.

One day I got a call from Red Owl. They were willing to go with Gold Bond if we were willing to give them the one-percent arrangement they were insisting on. We wanted to sign up a big chain awfully bad, but we were also convinced that we couldn't remain competitive with our arch-rival S & H with a one-percent agreement, so we decided to stall. I told Red Owl that we would have to think some more about the idea, and that I would get back to them in a day or two. Then I called Super Valu and told them that they'd have to decide one way or the other about Gold Bond because Red Owl had just made an offer.

To my relief—again I thank my lucky star—the Super Valu people told me to come out to their offices. They would assemble their Twin Cities managers and vote *yea* or *nay* while I waited in another room.

Well, you might be able to imagine the extreme sense of anticipation I felt while cooling my heels outside that Super Valu conference room! We had done everything they had permitted us to do in the way of selling our plan. Now there was nothing to do except wait.

It was, as best I could tell from my vantage point, one hell of a meeting. I could hear them pounding on the table and hollering at each other as though they were deciding on the fate of the Free World. Finally, Tom Harrison, Super Valu's chairman and president, came out and said, "You've got it. We'll try it out in Minneapolis." The vote in that conference room had been twenty-two for Gold Bond and only three against.

Just like that Super Valu, with hundreds of big supermarkets in the Twin Cities and across the country, had decided to become the first major chain to offer trading stamps. Not only that, they asked me, "How soon can we get started?" Once dead-set against stamps, now they wanted them yesterday.

Gold Bond was off to the races!

IT MAY BE DIFFICULT, some four decades later, to understand the impact that little trading stamp had on the retail food trade. I can assure you, however, with no fear of argument or contradiction, that there has never been, in history, a promotional program that ran longer or with more dramatic results.

Again, it didn't happen overnight. As excited as we were about the Super Valu campaign, we could only take things one step at a time. This was the break we'd been waiting for; we knew, for that matter, that every supermarket-chain executive in the nation would be watching. We simply had to take everything we knew about marketing and promotion, and, beginning at that April 1953 "grand opening," make everything function the way we said it would.

We gave it everything we had. We bought several pages worth of ads in the local papers, created and broadcast hundreds of jingles, sent out thousands of mailers, and trumpeted the Gold Bond-Super Valu connection across the airwaves. We pushed that grand opening the way we never pushed one before—and we succeeded. Those select Minneapolis-area Super Valu stores were jammed with shoppers responding to the hoopla and the lure of the stamps. The stores had trouble keeping their shelves full during the unprecedented stampede. I was on the scene, of course, watching and making mental note. I can't say the excitement I felt quite equaled the thrill that gripped me that wonderful March night back in 1938, when Arleen and I stood in front of Anfin Odland's little store with a flashlight and such great hope for the future—but, boy, it was close.

Of greater importance than that moment, though, would be the longer-range results. How would Super Valu—and Gold Bond—fare after the initial excitement faded, after the novelty of the stamp offering became an everyday routine? As it happened, we had an answer in less than a year. Within nine months of its initial offering of Gold Bond Stamps, Super Valu's business in Minneapolis had shot up by a whopping sixty-three percent!

Stamps, truly, were an idea whose time had come. Bear in mind, though, that the time was not very quick in coming. As I said before, fifteen years had elapsed between the founding of Gold Bond and the onset of the revolution sparked by that Super Valu sale. Fifteen years from beginning to breakthrough. Fifteen years to become an "overnight sensation."

The lesson, of course, is that while an entrepreneur need not be brilliant, he must be persistent. A wise man once said that the difference between success and failure is often only a matter of time. In countless cases, the successful entrepreneur is the one who hangs on a little longer than everybody else. He hangs on and hangs on, and one fine day, assuming he has some luck to go along with his persistence, he gets a break and he runs with it. Hanging on through all those lean years, we first perfected our idea. Through trial and error, we learned what we could—and couldn't—do with stamps. Then, when the time was right, we made the most of both our concept and experience.

I can't overestimate how hard we worked, always pushing and perfecting. The more we polished our presentation, the greater our percentage of sales to calls. The greater our percentage of sales to calls became, the more calls we made.

I spoke earlier about innovation and breakthrough. I had discovered the critical importance of innovation when I was just a kid selling newspapers, then had rediscovered it as a young man selling soap. Then, in the early '50s—nearing the age of forty and having so much more at stake—I rediscovered it yet again. The trading stamp was an old idea, but adapting it to the modern-day supermarket chain proved to be a breakthrough innovation.

And in 1954 I was playing for far more than I had ever played for in the past. The typical Gold Bond account at the time we landed Super Valu was good for about ten pads of stamps a month; in other words, a sale of about $145. All of a sudden I had in my hands a check, from a single account, worth a *quarter-of-a-million dollars!*

I can still remember staring at that check and realizing

that even above and beyond the incredible dollar value printed on its face, that single piece of paper was my ticket to the Major Leagues. Gold Bond was no longer an obscure little company struggling to sell an obscure little product for $145 at a crack. Gold Bond was "suddenly" in the big time, and its product was about to turn an industry on its head. The big number on that check was one thing, the potential it represented was quite another. I felt a tremendous thrill. I understood, at that point, that the sky might be the limit.

I knew, too, that our work had just begun.

CHAPTER EIGHT

Life in the Big Time

EVERY ENTREPRENEUR, at some point in his company's development, reaches a watershed, after which the way he does business is dramatically and forever changed.

Actually, the entrepreneur, over the span of a long career, faces a *series* of watersheds, each of which significantly alters his strategies and tactics, and sometimes changes even some heartfelt beliefs and long-cherished assumptions. It's just that the watershed at hand often seems so large and problematical that the others seem to pale by comparison.

Such was our decision, in 1953, to start redeeming trading stamps for gifts, or what we in the industry called premiums, instead of for cash, as we had been doing since our beginning in 1938. Super Valu insisted on the change, to be sure, but the truth is we would have gone to premiums on our own, without Super Valu's insistence, because by the early 1950s it had become clear that gifts were what the American housewife's love affair with the trading stamp was all about.

The evidence was mounting. One study, for instance, showed that savers in western Wisconsin—a state that prohibited the redemption of stamps for gifts—were regularly crossing the border into Minnesota to redeem their stamps for merchandise instead of cash. Polls and surveys from other parts of the country pointed to the same conclusion. Without much question, stamp savers simply preferred premiums to cash.

There was little mystery about that preference. Cash was cash—nothing less, nothing more. When a housewife brought home three dollar bills from a redemption center, that money was indistinguishable from the other money in the house, and more often than not quickly disappeared amid the family's petty cash. On the other hand, when a housewife brought home a shiny new toaster or a pretty new set of pillowcases, that gift was something that enhanced her home, impressed her neighbors, and told her family and friends that she was a smart and value-conscious shopper.

This involved a principle I'd learned many years earlier, when I received that gold wristwatch as a reward for my sales achievements at Procter & Gamble. That watch, as I've said, was worth so much more to me than any of the cash bonuses I received, because it served as continuing tangible evidence of my success. The bonus money was quickly spent; the watch, however, was for many years a source of pride, an ever-visible statement of my ability and accomplishments. It was also a powerful incentive to accomplish more.

You may wonder why, in light of that knowledge, Gold Bond hadn't redeemed stamps for gifts from the very start, why we waited for fifteen years before making the switch. The answer is simple: We couldn't afford to. A small stamp company—which, of course, is precisely what we'd been until landing that Super Valu account—could not afford to maintain a warehouse full of gifts, nor deal with all the logistical and personnel headaches that go with it.

Our business, in those early days, was blessedly simple. Each saver book full of stamps was good for $3 in cash or trade at any Gold Bond merchant. There were no warehouses, no redemption centers, no catalogs, no merchandise buyers, no shortages, no seasonal rushes, no customer complaints about wrong sizes, bad colors, and defective parts. (Yes, there was the long-running difficulty of safely disposing of the redeemed saver books, but we would have that problem no matter how we redeemed stamps.) I've often said, recalling those early years: Can you imagine such an idyllic company? All our assets were tied up in cash!

Idyllic companies, unfortunately, have a way of staying small and quiet, of becoming, in many cases, downright comatose. Our decision to go after the big supermarket chains was a decision to grow, to become a large, dynamic company, and to make tough choices. The time had come to borrow the money necessary to invest in all those fixed assets demanded by premium redemption.

To MAKE THE SWITCH to a gift-based stamp company, we suddenly needed additional office space as well as a warehouse and the first of a series of gift centers, a great number of new employees, not to mention an infusion of merchandising expertise, a catalog, and, of course, the gifts themselves.

It was an incredibly hectic period in our lives. We were not only converting the very basis of our business, but we were daily—*hourly,* it seemed—adding to the number of our accounts, as well as expanding and developing the accounts we already had. America's shoppers were hungry for stamps, and we had all we could do to keep up.

We eventually moved our headquarters to an erstwhile automobile-dealer's showroom at 1629 Hennepin Avenue, near the Basilica of St. Mary's Catholic Church, on the edge of downtown Minneapolis, and set up our first gift center in a one-time speakeasy at 400 Nicollet Avenue, where the Northern States Power building stands today. For the expertise as well as the premiums we turned to the firm of Cappel-MacDonald in Dayton, Ohio. From Elton MacDonald, the firm's savvy president, we very quickly learned a great deal about merchandising; from us MacDonald received an education in stamps. The exchange of knowledge would stand both of us in good stead for later events.

Our first gift catalog was a modest little publication featuring only about seventy-five items, which ranged from picnic baskets to electric mixers. A half book of Gold Bond stamps, according to that initial catalog, would get you a pair of lovely pillowcases; a complete book, a handsome cigarette lighter. As catalogs go, it wasn't exactly a work of art. But it got our gifts out in front of the public, and it brought in the eager savers. The response to that first catalog, in fact, was strong enough to allow us to develop our own warehouse and inventory. It's important to remember that we were once again breaking new ground. The Golden Age of Trading Stamps was just getting under way with stamps' acceptance by the big supermarket chains, and no one had yet written the gospel on the subject. We made plenty of mistakes. But, as always, we learned as much from our blunders as we learned from our breakthroughs. Probably a whole lot more.

We learned, for instance, that stamp savers wanted their premiums fast. For some of the larger items—an electric mixer, say, or a bridge lamp—they'd been dutifully pasting stamps into their saver books over the course of several weeks, thinking of the premium that awaited them. When they finally had the books filled, they were in no mood to wait another several weeks while the mixer was shipped out from the manufacturer back East. They could not go next door, to another "store," to "buy" that mixer, either. They were stuck with us, as it were, and they became understandably surly if we didn't have what they wanted when they wanted it.

At the same time, we discovered, perversely enough, that we could not make money if we stocked one-hundred percent of the items we carried in our catalog. Through the usual process of trial and error we finally understood that we could make our appropriate profit by maintaining a ninety-two-percent service level. That meant that out of every one hundred customers who came into one of our gift centers, ninety-two would get what they wanted. Anything above that ninety-two-percent level meant that we were overstocked, particularly in our slower-moving items. I said earlier that a successful entrepreneur is one who reduces, whenever possible, the size of his risks. That way he isn't putting all of his chips on a single roulette number that may never come up. So it was in the stamp business.

When we first switched over to gifts, we kept our risk to a minimum by purchasing our premiums from Cappel-Mac-Donald and working off the stock they were using for their own incentive programs. Their goods were not specifically tailored to the stamp trade, but in that first year after our transformation, redemption levels were relatively low and we were able to get by on the strength of their inventory. Eventually, following the publication of our catalog, we were able to generate sufficient income to allow us to support a warehouse full of premiums of our own. But we didn't want to make that move until we had the money to back it up.

We brought on a hard-working fellow named Warren Lorenz to ride herd on that part of the business. As our first real merchandise manager, Warren spent much of his day on the telephone with our various manufacturers, whose names were initially kept on a stack of file cards held together by a rubber band. He was also deeply involved in the publication of our second catalog, a slick, 16-page tabloid-size supplement that was tucked into the Sunday editions of the *Minneapolis Tribune* and *Des Moines Register*, as well as the *Dakota Farmer*, in August and September 1955.

In one fell swoop, Gold Bond's growing selection of desirable premiums was deposited on the front steps of 1.3-million households in four states. The response was tremendous. His first year at the task, Warren Lorenz, on a wing and a prayer, purchased merchandise worth $1.9 million. The following year—owing to the terrific demand—that total had tripled. Especially popular premiums included General Electric steam irons (for eleven and three-fourths books), Hamilton wristwatches, decorative bridge lamps, and several other household appliances on the high end of the book scale, eggbeaters and can openers (for a book apiece) on the low end. Most popular of all, though, were the sheets and pillowcases that Warren bought by the carload from the likes of Cannon Mills and Dan River, at low discount prices paid by the largest department stores. Gold Bond, in fact, became the largest single buyer of sheets and pillowcases in the entire Midwest.

As you might expect, the amount of volume we were beginning to generate gave us considerable leverage with most of the manufacturers we dealt with. We positioned ourselves as merchandise brokers, not wholesalers, and instead of getting, say, forty percent off on a particular item, we were able to wangle that discount to fifty.

The manufacturers gave us that additional break not because they loved us, but because we had learned how to deal, and, even more to the point, because they couldn't afford to live without the year-round exposure our catalogs were giving their products. Such, at that time, was the power and appeal of premium-based trading stamps.

O NCE PAST THAT CASH-TO-GIFT water-
shed, life in the big time really began to get interesting. As a matter of fact, if my life had gotten any more
interesting at one especially critical juncture in 1955, I
might have lost my shirt.

It was at that point that Cincinnati-based Kroger—then
the third-largest supermarket chain in the country, with
annual sales of more than a billion dollars—decided to get
into the trading stamp act. Kroger, you should understand,
was once among the most vociferous members of the anti-
stamp brigade. But times—and trends—had changed. As Joe
Hall, who was Kroger's chief executive at the time, remarked
on one occasion: "We fought them by cutting prices. We
gave away hosiery, dishes, and dolls. We used every gim-
mick known—and still the stamp stores took business away
from us. We couldn't fight them, so we joined them."

Having so decided, Kroger officials approached Elton
MacDonald, whose company, in nearby Dayton, had helped
them with a variety of incentive programs and contest premiums in the past. MacDonald, in turn, got hold of me
here in Minneapolis. He invited Gold Bond to join Cappel-MacDonald in a premium-based stamp agreement with
Kroger. You run the stamp part of the business, and we'll
take care of the premiums, he suggested. I told him we'd
think about his idea.

Some idea. At that time, we had signed up about forty
percent of the Super Valu stores across the country, with
our overall volume growing rapidly in a dozen or so states
as far away as California. We had a couple of dozen employees at our headquarters in Minneapolis and a couple of hundred persons scattered throughout the country. Our annual sales—up from $2.5 million before we landed the Super
Valu account—totaled $4.5 million. None of which, to the

cautious and prudent mind, made us large enough to go after a giant the size of Kroger.

My partner, Truman Johnson, possessed just such a cautious and prudent mind. Like me, he recognized the over-sized dimensions of the challenge. Like me, he understood that if we were to take on that Kroger account, we would, almost literally overnight, have to add a great number of new people, gift centers, and support facilities. Like me, he realized the incredible strain an account the size of Kroger would put on our resources—and on us, personally, as managers. *Un*like me, he was reluctant to take the plunge.

There were other hitches, too. Kroger, for one thing, wanted about a third of the stamp company in exchange for its business. Super Valu, for another, pointed out that it had exclusive use of Gold Bond Stamps in certain parts of the country—for instance, in Iowa and Wisconsin, where Kroger had stores. Super Valu's president, Tom Harrison, argued, quite correctly, that the Kroger account would result in a contractual conflict.

But I was increasingly eager to explore the possibilities as far and fast as I could. I went back to Tom Harrison and asked if Super Valu had any objections to our forming an entirely new stamp company, with an entirely new stamp. Surprised by the proposal, Harrison could find no good reason to stand in the way. Kroger officials, for their part, thought the idea was terrific. Furthermore, they suggested we bring in other non-competing chains and split the ownership of the new operation three ways. According to their plan, Kroger would own a third, the other participating chains would own a third, and Gold Bond would divide the remaining third with Cappel-MacDonald. First-year volume for this brand-new hybrid was projected to be in the neighborhood of $90 million.

Still, it was a nerve-wracking period. At Gold Bond we agonized over the many possible ramifications of the proposed arrangement. Developing those Super Valu accounts had taken virtually every ounce of energy and resource we had at the time. Now we wondered how much more of our precious resources—human, financial, and logistical— would have to be expended in the assembly of the new operation. We asked ourselves if we were risking everything we had worked so hard to build up over the past decade-and-a-half by creating a new company that would, in effect, be competing against it.

Truman urged caution. We had a good thing going, he argued, so why rock the boat and risk swamping it? To me, however, there was no real safety in the status quo. As far as I was concerned, the only way to make sure we'd be in business tomorrow (not to mention the day after that) was to grow, to expand, to make the most of every opportunity presented to us.

Finally, Truman and I agreed that we'd pursue the new deal—though we agreed with sharply differing levels of enthusiasm.

AND THERE WERE STILL MORE HITCHES. For instance, we had no sooner decided to call the new entry the "Thank You" Stamp when we learned that a tobacconist in Washington, D.C., had for many years been giving out Thank You coupons with the sale of cigarettes. The tobacconist held the rights to the name and asked us for $10,000 in exchange for our using it. We thought the name was great and therefore agreed to the figure, but at that point the fellow, sensing our eagerness, upped his price to $15,000. When we agreed to the new figure, the guy hesitated again and insisted on, in addition to the $15,000, two percent of gross sales on all Thank You Stamps. I told him to hell with it.

We tried to come up with a new name, but had little success. "Thank You" had been perfect—short, direct, and personable —and everything else seemed flat by comparison. Eventually, my friend and legal counsel, Matthew Levitt, started calling the new company "Top Value" for want of anything better, and the name, like the stamp itself, stuck.

Meanwhile, the exploratory talks among the various potential partners had gotten down to bedrock bargaining. Now that kind of hard-nosed negotiation is something I happen to be pretty good at. I do my homework and know what I want, and I don't let myself be distracted by side issues. What's more, I'm a stubborn Swede who cut his teeth at Procter & Gamble, and therefore know how to be tough and hang in there.

Despite all that, though, the talks had reached an impasse. Kroger's negotiators were tough, too, and more experienced than we were, and they had come to the point where they decided to dig in their heels. We were insisting on a twenty-cent-a-pad fee, to be split with Cappel-MacDonald for developing and operating the Top Value program. Kroger said they would give us only ten cents a pad. That one thin dime's difference was the sole subject of discussion during two separate meetings in Cincinnati.

A third meeting was convened in Dayton. But neither side was willing to budge, and so, to all intents and purposes, the negotiations were over. The deal was off. Kroger's men headed for the airport, while our team repaired to the Van Cleve Hotel bar.

Sitting in that bar, I tried to come up with a way to salvage the plan. I pulled out a pencil and hurriedly began scribbling figures on a pad. I wondered: If we conceded to

Kroger the ten-cent-a-pad provision—obviously the key to a settlement—how could we make up the difference that we knew we needed? Could we get fifty cents a pad instead of twenty-five from the several other, smaller accounts in the deal? I decided it was worth a try.

I hurried to the phone and had Roy Godley, who headed the Kroger team, paged at the airport. I ran my idea past him. Godley chatted a moment with one of his teammates, then said it was fine with them. As far as Kroger was concerned, we could charge the other accounts as much as we could get.

"That's all I need to know," I replied. "We have ourselves a deal!"

CHAPTER NINE

Solo and Safeway

OUR INVOLVEMENT WITH KROGER and the Top Value stamp program lasted less than a year. Our withdrawal from the program after so brief a period might have represented a major defeat if I hadn't come away from the deal wiser, wealthier, and, a short while later, free to fly solo again.

To no one's surprise, developing and servicing the Top Value account put a tremendous strain on everybody. The Top Value program, as it was finally established, encompassed not only Kroger, but a number of other, smaller, noncompeting supermarket chains, including Stop & Shop in Boston, Penn Fruit in Philadelphia, Hart's in New York State, Hinky Dinky in Nebraska, and Humpty Dumpty in Oklahoma—the top regional names in the supermarket industry. It took nearly everything and everyone we had to get all those accounts up and running.

Cappel-MacDonald had agreed to take care of the premium end of the venture. To handle the new business on the stamp side I needed no fewer than three hundred additional salespeople. Several of our crack Gold Bond supervisors—fellows like Vern McCoy, Bob Thorpe, and Les Owens—were transferred, on a temporary basis, to Top Value. Gold Bond was practically stripped of experienced stamp personnel to enable us to stay on top of the burgeoning Top Value sales. The need for new personnel, particularly men who could sell, had grown far beyond our capability. We hired as many of our more talented, aggressive acquaintances as possible—another one of my brothers, Warren, was brought on at that time—and then counted heavily on the use of want ads in the papers. I hired a man named Elmer Wheeler, a charismatic Texan well-known in sales circles at the time, to head up a crash training program for the new recruits.

We launched the new program in Indianapolis, where the local Kroger division was struggling against another tough stamp program, and we quickly helped that division turn the tide. Then just as quickly we set up Top Value programs in several other Kroger divisions, including Detroit, where the chain's local managers had once been staunchly opposed to stamps. In less than a year we could point with justifiable pride—and with some shortness of breath!—to a soaring Kroger sales volume as well as proportionately impressive gains among the other chains participating in the program. Top Value's sales boomed from $1 billion to $1.45 billion in less than ten months.

While Truman Johnson was minding Gold Bond's business at home, I was spending most of my time on the road, selling that Top Value plan as hard as I possibly could. I felt, as I always did when I was selling, a tremendous exhilaration. I was a salesman, after all, and to me there was no greater thrill than selling a new account. But it was terribly hectic, and I was spending virtually six out of seven days on the road, away from Gold Bond and my family in Minneapolis.

My operating principle was to travel by night and work during the day, and I spent so many crazy hours going in and out of airports that I'd occasionally be hard-pressed to tell someone exactly where I was. Dee Kemnitz, my nearly infallible secretary at the time, would prepare a pink slip with my itinerary on it before every trip, and that little piece of paper would be my absolutely indispensable guide. But even with that, I would sometimes find myself wondering. . . .

I remember one night calling Dee from a tiny airport somewhere in Ohio. "Dee," I asked her, "do you know where I am?"

Dee replied: "Yes, I know where you are."

"Good," I said. "Then maybe you can tell me how I *got* here."

I was tired and frustrated by all the inefficient puddle-jumping that was necessary in order to complete my appointed rounds. At the same time, I understood that in 1956, before the era of the executive jet, there was simply no better alternative if we wanted to develop the business.

And developing that business we were. Our management fees were soaring to levels appropriate to the amount of business Top Value was generating for Kroger and their supermarket partners; indeed, those fees had risen into the hundreds of thousands of dollars. But those fees had risen so high so fast that Kroger officials began to object to the contract as "unconscionable," and they threatened to sue to break it. They wanted to reduce the 10 cents we earned on every $550 in grocery sales even further. When we refused to accept a lesser commission, they offered to buy us out of the contract.

Elton MacDonald was amenable to picking up his profit and moving on. So was Truman Johnson, who had not been very enthusiastic about the arrangement in the first place. The notion of selling out, though, stuck in my craw. I believed that a fellow doesn't have to be the smartest man in the world to be successful, but he does have to have the guts to hang in there when the going gets tough. Besides, I argued, sales were booming. After we'd worked so hard to get Top Value up and running, why shouldn't we ride a winner?

Our counsel, Matthew Levitt, advised us to hang tough, arguing that Kroger had little chance of winning any such lawsuit. I proposed we give Kroger a choice of alternatives, either one of which would be acceptable to me: We continue to manage Top Value, or they buy us out at $4 million.

A S IT HAPPENED, Kroger agreed to buy us out at that "astronomical" number. Thus Truman and I, with our collective one-half of the Top Value pie, each came away from that short-lived arrangement with a million dollars for our trouble. And speaking of astronomy, I must once again give credit to my lucky star, because without that Top Value buy-out I might never have gotten back one hundred percent of my original company.

Truman, you'll recall, held fifty percent of the Gold Bond stock. He had been brought in during the middle of the war and given half the ownership when it appeared that I would be drafted. If the truth be told, under ordinary circumstances I would never have given anyone half the store, nor would I recommend such a move, under ordinary circumstances, to any other entrepreneur. But bringing in a partner seemed to be the only prudent course of action at the time, and Truman turned out to be a congenial coequal. He was honest and forthright, a good salesman and an effective manager. We worked hard together to bring our business back and increase it after the war, and together we shared the rewards that followed our landing of the Super Valu and Kroger accounts. Despite all the strain and pressures, I can't recall there ever being a harsh word between us.

By the middle 1950s, however, Truman and I were operating under fundamentally different philosophies. By that time Truman, who was roughly ten years my senior, had reached a level of accomplishment and reward that seemed to suit him just fine. Gold Bond was robustly successful, and he had become a wealthy man. Thinking about retiring early and moving to California, he was averse to taking additional risks, to jeopardizing what was already a profitable operation, to breaking his neck for the sake of continued (and, to him, unnecessary) growth. I, on the other hand, was still very hungry. I was still eager to accept new risks, and I was absolutely convinced that the alternative to growth is to wither on the vine.

Curiously enough, we had never determined which of us would be Gold Bond's chief executive officer. All that we'd ever decided was that Truman would bear the title of chairman while I would be called president, and that we would split the responsibilities as best suited our respective talents and temperaments. Truman, for the most part, was content to stay put at the home office and keep track of the paperwork. I couldn't wait to get out there in the hustle and bustle of the marketplace and sell from morning to night.

Well, that division of labor worked well enough for more than a decade. Then, about the time of the Top Value settlement, it became obvious to both of us that we had reached a parting of the way.

One day, sitting on Truman's boat in the middle of Lake Minnetonka on the outskirts of Minneapolis, we talked about the future of the Gold Bond Stamp Company. Our differences were immediately apparent, particularly on the issue of growth. Truman said, in effect, that I was setting the company's sights too high, that our goals were too ambitious, and that he was unhappy with the fast pace and expansion-oriented direction in which the company was pointed. I replied that I was determined to see the company grow as fast and as large as possible, and that, as far as I was concerned, an entrepreneur could never afford to rest on past achievements. I also told him that while I was not about to get out of the stamp business, I would be willing to make him a buy or sell offer and he could choose which option he wanted at the price I had set. He told me to go ahead and make him such an offer.

We struggled over the details of a settlement for a couple of weeks. I told him, early in our discussions, that if he chose to buy me out, I would go to California and start over. If I bought him out, I told him, I wouldn't object to his getting back in the business so long as he stayed out of the immediate five-state area for one year. He said he didn't want to start another company, that what he really wanted to do was settle down and live off the fruits of his labor.

Finally, we got together with our lawyers. The price I set at which I would buy or sell was $1 million. Truman said that he wanted to sell, but that the price was too low; he insisted on a quarter-of-a-million dollars more. I knew he was playing poker and I could call his bluff. But the prospect of staying in Minneapolis with the Gold Bond organization intact was too strong for me to resist. I felt his demand was a betrayal of our original agreement, but I was eager to get my company back. I was also very eager to get back to work. I agreed to pay Truman his million dollars in cash and, as he insisted, to pay him an additional $50,000 annually over the following five years. The deal was struck.

True to his instincts, Truman went home, sold his house, and retired with his wife to California. True to my own, I got back to work.

THE SETTLEMENT with Truman Johnson all but cleaned me out. The nest egg I had put together from the sale of Top Value was used to close the deal. I did have, however, my precious Gold Bond Stamp Company, which I had founded and nurtured from birth. Probably even more important, I was once again independent. I had the freedom to fly as high, far, and fast as I could.

People have asked me: If I could do it over again, would I come to the same decision and buy my partner out for all that money, or would I let him buy me out and start from scratch? Honestly, I'm not sure. On the one hand, I was still a young man—I was only forty-three years old in 1957 with plenty of get up and go. Furthermore, I knew the stamp business as well as anyone in the country by that stage in my career, and I have no doubt that I would have succeeded with a whole new operation. On the other, under the terms of our settlement, I was able to stay put in Minneapolis, my hometown, and build on a tried-and-true foundation— my organization. And I was once again my own man. After fourteen years of sharing it with a partner, all the responsibility and authority were back where I always believed they should be: smack-dab in the middle of my desk.

As far as I was concerned, I couldn't have gotten back sole ownership of the company at a more propitious time. Gold Bond was once again on the track of big game—the *biggest* game, in fact, in the supermarket jungle—Safeway Foods.

In the middle 1950s, Safeway, with supermarkets primarily in the West and Southwest, and A & P, whose stores were situated mostly in the East, were the two largest chains in the nation. Both, historically, had been adamantly opposed to trading stamps. Lingan Warren, Safeway's long-time president, had told me in so many words to stay away from the chain's Oakland, California, headquarters. "Don't come out here," he said bluntly. "If you do come out here, don't come

to the office. If you do come to the office, I won't see you."
And when Warren was replaced in the face of the chain's
declining volume, his successor, Robert Magowan, was no
more hospitable. Magowan, in fact, quickly posted a reward
of one-million dollars payable to anyone who could come
up with a viable alternative to stamps.

Nonetheless, in 1957 I discovered a chink in the previously impenetrable Safeway armor with the unexpected
help of a fellow by the name of Maurie Gold. Maurie was
a pawnbroker in El Paso, Texas, at the time, and he'd learned
that the local Safeway division was getting soundly trounced
by its stamp-giving competition. En route to Minneapolis
to visit his mother one day, Maurie happened to sit next to
my sister Aileen on the airplane. In the course of their casual conversation Aileen mentioned that I was in the trading-
stamp business. Maurie was intrigued by what he'd heard
about stamps. So, upon arriving in Minneapolis, he called
me and arranged an interview.

When we met in my office Maurie excitedly advised me
that Safeway, once the leading grocery chain in El Paso, was
now a poor second. Another chain, Furr's, was eating Safeway's lunch, so to speak, by issuing trading stamps, and Safeway's counter-promotions had been failures. Then Maurie
asked me if he could call on the chain's El Paso division manager on behalf of Gold Bond. Figuring there was nothing to
lose through Maurie's initiative, I told him to go right ahead.

Maurie returned to El Paso and contacted the local Safeway division manager, Dave Kimball. Kimball did not like
the idea of stamps any better than his superiors at Safeway
headquarters in Oakland, but he knew only too well that
his division was in serious trouble. He agreed to meet with
Maurie. When Maurie reported that the manager was, if
not exactly enthusiastic about the prospect of stamps, at

least amenable to further conversation, I immediately flew down to Texas and met with Kimball myself. Eventually, with the reluctant approval of the Safeway brass, the El Paso manager agreed to experiment with Gold Bond.

The El Paso division, with its fifty-eight supermarkets in west Texas and New Mexico, was not such an enormous prize in and of itself. But it was obvious to me what an opportunity that "little" outfit presented to us. If Gold Bond did well down there, the entire Safeway empire would sit up and take notice. As big as the Super Valu and Kroger accounts had been, Safeway, with more than 2,100 stores throughout the country, would be the grandest prize yet.

Once given the go-ahead, we mounted a full-scale blitz of El Paso and its environs. We hit 150,000 homes in the area with a package containing an explanatory letter from the local Safeway store manager, a Gold Bond saver's book with a hundred complimentary stamps, and a number of coupons redeemable for additional stamps. Not only that, but we shouted the Gold Bond message from dozens of billboards and sang it in a series of radio and television commercials. Three-page newspaper ads, bus signs, and even a battalion of pretty young women dressed in Sandy Saver outfits made sure that no one between El Paso and Albuquerque was unaware that Gold Bond Stamps were now available at the nearby Safeway.

To complement the promotional hoopla, we sent in two teams of twenty-three of our best salespeople, all of whom would cover the territory in rented station wagons filled with store signs, posters, and other materials. Vern McCoy was assigned to head up the blitz in El Paso. Another seasoned Gold Bond veteran, Don Hackett, was sent to Midland-Odessa, and my brother Dean was dispatched to Albuquerque. I personally spent the better part of the summer and fall of 1957 commuting between Minneapolis and west Texas, along with several of my top lieutenants. All of my attention was focused on the fast-approaching "grand opening" scheduled for October 1st.

As I was confident it would, the tremendous amount of planning, expense, and effort paid off. We hit pay dirt in Safeway's El Paso territory. Sales at many of the participating markets jumped a spectacular one-hundred percent following that blitz; the territory as a whole was averaging heady gains of forty percent. Associate accounts in the region eventually totaled two-hundred-one—one more than the ambitious goal I had set for our sales force.

As a reward for his efforts in the El Paso breakthrough, Maurie Gold was named division manager in that area and later was a super salesman-at-large in charge of special projects as far away as Great Britain.

I next turned my attention to Safeway headquarters in California, where I was sure a billion-dollar empire awaited me.

CHAPTER TEN

The Flying Squadron

AT PARTICULARLY TRYING TIMES in our development, I used to buck up my top men and women by telling them, "This company thrives on problems. If the challenge wasn't so difficult, people with less ability would be taking our business."

That was not just casual cheerleading, nor merely another twist on the old "When the going gets tough, the tough get going" bromide. I believed what I was telling my executives during those wild growth years of the mid-1950s, and I believe it to this day. Call them what you will—problems, challenges, obstacles, hurdles. By any name, they are the elements that stimulate the entrepreneur's imagination, strengthen his resolve, reinforce his discipline, and refine his technique. In the end, if he's conquered them, they will sweeten the entrepreneur's success as well.

Such a challenge was giant Safeway. Despite our breakthrough in its El Paso division, I discovered, to my considerable surprise and consternation, that the big chain's top brass, headquartered in Oakland, had not been won over to the notion of trading stamps. In fact, the company's official policy, I was told, continued to be decidedly *anti*-stamp.

I was soon to find out, however, that the company had been impressed by our performance in Texas, and that it might be worth our while to mount a campaign in its

Phoenix, Arizona, division. Safeway's stores, I discovered upon my own investigation, had fallen into second place in the Phoenix market. In an attempt to regain their former dominance, the local Safeways were pushing a "Premium of the Month" promotion involving cash-register tapes and rotating prizes. But the promotion, I learned further, wasn't very popular with the public (or, for that matter, with individual store managers, who had to stock the prizes themselves) and thus not particularly effective as a means of boosting sales. I acknowledged the challenge, all right; I also saw, beyond the challenge, another tremendous opportunity.

Having completed our investigation (today we call it "market research"), we decided to focus our attention on Phoenix. Safeway's top man there agreed, albeit reluctantly, to let us state our case in front of the division's individual store managers. *Us*, at that point, was yours truly and a new fellow—a hard-driving former hardware salesman from Duluth named Harry Greenough. Together Harry and I put on a dog-and-pony show that might have made a pair of vaudevillians proud—or done them in, out of sheer exhaustion.

We worked like hell on that presentation and left nothing either to chance or the viewer's imagination. We used a carrousel slide projector (at that time, state-of-the-art audio-visual), plus graphs, charts, and a glittering assortment of gifts arrayed about us on stage to suggest a Gold Bond gift center. Amid all the props and promotional materials, Harry and I maintained a swift and lively stream of persuasive commentary and explanation, one or the other of us "on" for five or six minutes at a time, telling the managers how Gold Bond Stamps would make their stores Number One again. The managers were also treated to a first-class lunch and given Sandy Saver cuff links and cigarette lighters. And at the show's completion the managers were invited to pick their own door prizes from the display onstage until the shelves were bare.

This, of course, is a necessarily abbreviated account of what went on down there. The research, preparation, and presentation itself—not to mention the larger territorial sales effort that followed—involved a good deal of dollars, man-hours, and old-fashioned hard work. "Inspiration and perspiration" is what we called it back then, and that's as good a description of our recipe for success as I can think of. It was, to say the least, a huge investment of the company's resources, but its net effect was to make believers out of the Safeway people in Arizona.

Gold Bond Stamps were given out in the region's twenty-five Safeway stores beginning in January 1958.

OUR OPENING of Safeway's El Paso division had provided us with invaluable experience for the opening of Phoenix. We'd made mistakes in Texas, to be sure, but we had learned—and thereby profited—from most of them. We knew, too, that beyond Phoenix lay the other big outposts of the Safeway empire, including Kansas City, Omaha, Little Rock, Denver, and New York City. Thus, it seemed obvious that what we'd learned in El Paso and put to work in Phoenix would stand us in good stead when we went after Safeway's business elsewhere. It also seemed obvious that our ordinary way of opening a new territory was no longer going to be sufficient if we wanted to make the most out of our Safeway initiative.

Clearly, we needed to refine and develop the blitz concept we'd put together on an *ad hoc* basis in El Paso. We needed a group—a special force—of highly trained, highly motivated, highly mobile people who, once we'd established a beachhead, could swoop down, literally out of the clear blue sky, and capture the entire territory. Such a force, like a crack commando unit, would be prepared to fly anywhere on short notice, sign up new accounts, then turn the operation of those accounts over to a permanent crew and withdraw to prepare for its next deployment.

Once the idea of such a group had been worked out, I appointed an aggressive account manager by the name of Orville Hammer to be in charge of its operation. I tapped my brother Warren to be out on the unit's "point," in charge of scouting and recruitment. The unit itself was originally called the Development Squad, though that name did not do justice to the excitement it generated among its members. They called themselves "crash crews," and dubbed the group the "Flying Squadron."

Whatever they called themselves, they earned their wings in that Phoenix campaign. There, as they would elsewhere, they concentrated on associate accounts: a drugstore, service station, gift shop, lumber yard—virtually any legitimate commercial establishment they could sign up as part of a neighborhood shopping area—anchored, of course, on a Safeway market. And they were wildly successful. Phoenix, despite the initial opposition, took to Gold Bond stamps to an extent that undoubtedly surprised everybody except us diehard believers. Not the least surprised was Robert Magowan, Safeway's president, out in Oakland. Magowan called our Phoenix success nothing short of "amazing"—and described the Arizona capital as the most "stamp-conscious city" in the country.

From "stamp-conscious" Phoenix the Flying Squadron moved on to Little Rock, Arkansas, and then Denver, Colorado, by which time the unit had been expanded to six crews of a dozen men apiece. Denver would be the Squadron's biggest test to date, comprising as it did the largest and most profitable of all of Safeway's divisions. The Denver territory included no fewer than one-hundred-fifty-eight Safeway stores scattered across five Rocky Mountain states and generated no less than $200 million in annual sales.

Warren Carlson, the Squadron's "point man," had gone in first, rented the requisite fleet of cars, recruited the additional "soldiers" we would need, and staked out our targets in the huge Denver region that stretched all the way from the western Dakotas to northern New Mexico. He also arranged for the use of an enormous old house not far from downtown Denver to serve as both a central staging area and a barracks for thirty men. That old house—with its boarded-over swimming pool in the basement and its stable-turned-storage building out in back—would forever be known among Gold Bond veterans as "the Mansion."

When the Flying Squadron descended upon Denver, salesmen were brought in from all over the country to help with the blitz. We attracted, as might be expected, our fair share of eccentrics and other less-than-desirable candidates. Old hands may recall one fellow who carried a Confederate flag and umbrella wherever he went, and another who insisted on making sales calls accompanied by his pet canaries. Still another fellow was terrified of driving, and rang up $400 worth of taxi fares before he was relieved of his duties and sent home.

To the Mansion in Denver came the good, the bad, and the indifferent. In the basement "ballroom" where once there had been a pool, the recruits were given their detailed orientation, instructions, and pep talk. The Squadron's chief, Orville Hammer, quickly culled the bad and indifferent from among the good and provided them with additional training; if that didn't do the trick, they were given a plane ticket back to whence they'd come. Those who stayed were stacked in like cordwood. They slept as many as six to a room, fought among themselves for use of the Mansion's two bathrooms, and groused about the "house rules" prohibiting strong drink and female visitors. At least one man complained that he'd "had it better in the Army."

But once again the Squadron worked hard—and worked wonders. Denver was another success. So, in rapid procession, were Omaha, Dallas, Kansas City, and Tulsa. Taking on a new division every six weeks or so, the Squadron was speedily turning Safeway territory into Gold Bond country. Finally it was time to set our sights on New York City, Safeway's biggest market east of the Mississippi River.

If there were ever any doubt about it, our experience quickly dispelled it: *New York City ain't Omaha.* From the dog-and-pony show that Harry Greenough and I put on for Safeway's local managers in the club room of a local brewery to the various breakdowns, delays, and snafus encountered during our subsequent blitz, our New York City experience was, to say the least, unique.

Picture, for example, a phalanx of Safeway managers, beer mugs in hand, marching to the music of a brass band around a room full of kegs and spigots. Picture a caravan of rented Edsels piled high with Gold Bond paraphernalia getting stuck—because the paraphernalia was piled *too* high—in the Lincoln Tunnel. Picture Orville Hammer manning the phones at the Squadron's temporary headquarters in nearby Jersey City, trying to calm or reorient the dozens of troops who were calling in lost, overheated, or otherwise discombobulated by the pressures of the Big Apple.

For sixteen weeks the Flying Squadron worked the New

York City territory, and, I can assure you, there was never a dull moment. There was, however, new evidence to support the old saw that a salesman who could sell in New York could sell anywhere.

When all was said and done, those fellows in the Flying Squadron could produce wherever they went. Their operating philosophy was "Don't sell in singles, sell in bunches," and that's exactly what they did. They fought off fatigue and homesickness. They operated under intense pressure and overcame whatever anti-stamp resistance they encountered in the field. When they sold one division, they moved on to the next, leaving a permanent crew to follow through on their efforts and service the new accounts. They themselves just kept on selling.

Despite the pressure and fatigue, the Squadron's morale always seemed high. For one thing, they were selling what was, at that time, a red-hot product. In the mid- and late-1950s, trading stamps were all but irresistible. We would go into a supermarket division that was accounting for, say, $100 million in sales and get that division up to $150 million or more in less than a year with those stamps. For another, they were driven, like all successful salesmen, by the pride of their achievement. They would stand up in front of their peers every night and report how much they'd sold that day, and they would be rewarded with prizes and a whole lot of whoop-dee-doo. The next morning they'd be champing at the bit to get back out there.

FROM MY POINT OF VIEW, that kind of relentless, hard-charging attitude and behavior was absolutely essential to our continuing success. I demanded as much and expected no less. In 1957, when I had regained complete control of my company, I set a sales goal of five-million pads of stamps by 1961. That meant a hundred-percent increase every year for the next five years, and *that* meant nothing less than one-hundred-percent concentration, dedication, and hard work.

Then as now, we believed in goals—measurable, flexible, useful goals. Through the use of goals we knew what we were doing and where we were going, and nothing could divert us. I had learned, moreover, that the proper application of goals was the most effective method of motivating my organization, from the top all the way down to the bottom. "Obstacles," I would tell our people again and again, "are those frightening things you see when you take your eyes off the goal. Keep your eyes fixed steadfastly on that goal, and you'll never be confused, distracted, or defeated."

We also believed in our people. We believed in making our people realize their important responsibility and worth to the company. As a matter of fact, we had a saying—a creed, really—that we repeated en masse at our annual meetings. "The future of this company," it said aloud, "lies in the minds and hearts of the people in this room."

I had by this time established an Executive Committee to oversee the entire, ever-widening scope of the Gold Bond organization. The committee consisted of Joe Hunt, Harry Greenough, and our four territorial managers—Warren Carlson, Vern McCoy, Dean Carlson, and Lloyd Thompson—all of whom had been promoted to vice presidencies. We met, the seven of us, one Saturday every month. No excuses were allowed for absence, and no one was permitted to leave until we had finished. If a meeting ran too late into Saturday afternoon, it was continued the following Monday morning.

Those meetings were intense. Just as I expected a total commitment from my sales force, I expected it also from my top-most executives. I confess, too, that then as now I hated to be told I was wrong. There would sometimes be a little shouting and some banging on the table—but, despite occasional rumors to the contrary, there was rarely any bloodshed.

The real enemy, at that point, was complacency. Thanks, in large measure, to the astonishing effectiveness of our Flying Squadron, the company was growing incredibly fast. By the end of the decade, Gold Bond was employing almost seven-hundred persons and operating nearly two-hundred gift centers around the country. Our total sales were approaching the $50-million level. We were exceeding our annual quotas every year, and that five-million-pad goal was drawing closer by the day. We might have been excused if we had relaxed a little, eased ourselves into low gear, and allowed ourselves to think, "Well, we've made it. Enough is enough." But we didn't. We *wouldn't*. Not then, not ever. Not if I had anything to say about it—which, of course, I did.

I insisted that we in management set high standards of performance for ourselves. I insisted that we eat, sleep, and breathe Gold Bond business—six, even seven days a week. Moreover, I gave our salespeople and their supervisors an ultimatum. They could either ease up and become unpromotable, or they could expend additional energy, overcome whatever obstacles lay between them and the goal, and strive to reach new heights with the company.

And, believe me, I left them absolutely no doubt as to which course of action I expected them to choose.

CHAPTER ELEVEN

The Need to Diversify

IFIRMLY BELIEVE that an entrepreneur needs only one good idea to make it big in America. The market here—as compared with, say, Sweden, Germany, and many other European countries—is so large and so dynamic that there will always be enough people to "buy" your good idea and, so doing, make you a success.

It needn't be a complicated or exotic idea, either; generally speaking, I'd go so far as to say the simpler, the better. The simpler it is, the easier it is to explain to a banker or venture capitalist, and then to your sales force and, finally, through your sales force, to the buying public. Furthermore, the simpler it is, the easier it ought to be to improve and perfect.

At Gold Bond, the central idea was always simple: Take the trading stamp—itself a wonderfully uncomplicated concept—and apply it to the retail food business. For more than twenty years we concentrated on that single idea. For more than twenty years we did everything we could think of to expand, extend, and improve it—and we became a dominant force not only in the stamp industry, but in the retail grocery industry as well.

We were always looking for new ways to enhance the basic idea. The development of the associate-account concept, which I described earlier in the book, is an obvious example of that kind of enhancement. So was the deployment of the Flying Squadron and the use of such aggressive marketing plans as the very popular Treasure Chest and Sandy Saver Dial-a-Mile promotions. In some instances, the enhancements had themselves been around for a while. As Harry Greenough, who for years was in charge of our various promotions, once explained it, "We'll take an old idea, dress it up, give it a new name, and put our manpower and expertise behind it." That "old idea" would then be as good as new—or better.

A good example of this idea-recycling process was our adaptation of an old Procter & Gamble chestnut called "Cash for Your Church." Under the plan (which I first encountered during my soap-selling days), P & G had "paid back" half a cent for every Oxydol box top and Ivory soap wrapper sent in by a participating church group, thereby enhancing its sales and establishing a little good will by helping out a worthy cause. We dusted off that old P & G idea, created a new Group Projects division to run it, and reached out not only to church groups, but to parent-teacher associations, Elks and Kiwanis auxiliaries, and dozens of other legitimate, nonprofit organizations throughout the country. Group Projects chief Sherle Lowe, assisted by such effective saleswomen as Fay McCall and, for a time, my daughter Marilyn, then proceeded to organize hundreds of kaffe klatsches around the country. In those cheerful, upbeat, informal settings, they explained how the plan worked and enlisted the enthusiastic aid of thousands of volunteers.

The promotion was a model of simplicity in its own right. For every Gold Bond saver's book validated on behalf of a participating organization, the housewife received a gift and her group was given points toward its own objective. This often paid for a roof repair or refurbished facility. A trip to Jerusalem was presented to many a pastor by his thrifty, stamp-saving congregation. The promotion was also a model of popular success. Fay McCall (who succeeded Sherle Lowe) and her staff eventually had upwards of 600,000 women taking part in the plan. More than a hundred schools earned new buses through the program, and at least one Baptist congregation acquired a new Cessna airplane to help with its mission work. Gold Bond, in the process, discovered for itself the awesome power of group sales.

Adding to your market is one thing; enhancing your existing product or service—that is, your basic idea—in order to exploit that market is another. The entrepreneur, if he wishes to get and stay ahead of the pack, must constantly find ways to accomplish both.

I never thought there was a lot of choice. It seemed to me you either found new ways to add to and enhance your business, or you slipped behind and, eventually, fell by the wayside. Furthermore, the stamp business was always relatively cheap and easy to enter; I started, as you'll recall, as a part-time entrepreneur with only $55 in (borrowed) capital! Thus you had to keep growing and coming up with new or recycled enhancements as a means not just of staying ahead of the current competition, but of discouraging or inhibiting new competition from developing any momentum.

Besides, let us not forget that it is that combined imperative of continuing growth and ongoing innovation that keeps your work interesting, invigorating, and fun.

BY 1960, THE SIMPLE TRADING STAMP had made me successful far beyond my expectations. It had taken me, as an entrepreneur, into the heady realm of big business, and had allowed me, as a provider, to give my wife and children a quality of life my parents could scarcely have imagined. Small wonder, then, that I loved the stamp business, that I couldn't wait to get to the office in the morning, that I refused to let up in my quest to grow Gold Bond bigger and stronger.

Today, in the age of the multifaceted conglomerate, it may seem quaint to say, but once we were up and really running, I never gave much serious consideration to branching out into other fields. Nor did I ever think seriously about taking the money out of stamps and plunging into a brand-new venture, or slipping into an early retirement, or becoming a part-time, hands-off executive whose afternoons were devoted to the perfection of his golf game.

No, for almost a quarter of a century, I was single-minded in my devotion to the Gold Bond Stamp Company, its continuing growth, and its increasing prosperity. From the time I arrived at work in the morning until the time I went home at night, I gave it one-hundred percent of my attention.

I remember a friend of mine, a terrific salesman in his day who had become the president of a large publicly held company, once saying to me: "Curt, I just don't understand you. You can't come out and play golf even one afternoon a week. Why, I get out on the golf course everyday, and my company is a hell of a lot bigger than yours."

"It's true," I remember telling him, "I just can't seem to find the time it requires."

My friend said, "There's *plenty* of time. I get my day's work done in two hours."

"How do you that?" I asked.

He said, "It's simple. You just go down to the office every morning, go through your mail, decide what goes to whom, then let your people run the show. You get out of there and go play golf."

Well, it sounded kind of nice all right—but, to my way

of thinking, highly impractical and even dangerous as well. And, as it happened, all that time on the golf course eventually—I would say inevitably—cost my friend's company a great deal in lost opportunity and cost my friend his job. The fact is, a chief executive can delegate only so much, and his subordinates can exercise their authority only so far. The CEO must keep his eye on the big picture and be available to make the big decisions that only he can make. That kind of top-level activity requires his full-time attention. As long as his name sits on the top of the corporate directory, he needs to be there, on or about or at least in close touch with the premises—not out, footloose and fancy free, on the sixteenth green at the club.

I was never very interested in early retirement, either. The thought of playing golf or tennis all day was no more enthralling to me than the thought of playing it every afternoon. I suppose I was simply not brought up to lie about and take life easy. As much as I enjoy a good time, I have never been very comfortable with extended stretches of idleness. Besides, I was healthy and still very much in my prime. I loved going to work every day at the age of forty-six as much as I did at the age of twenty-three. So why on earth would I want to give up having so much fun and miss the excitement of the business arena?

At Gold Bond there was always plenty of excitement. By 1960 we were beginning to extend our markets abroad. Five years earlier we had become the first United States-based trading-stamp company with an international division. That had been established to oversee our operations in Canada (with the I.G.A. stores), a number of islands in the Caribbean, and, later, the United Kingdom, continental Europe, and Japan.

Each foray into a foreign country seemed to present its

own peculiar challenge. I recall, during the middle '50s, when Bertram Loeb walked into my office. He said that if I could find a legal way to bring stamps into Canada, he would like to have I.G.A. stores handle them exclusively in his territory. The hitch was a Canadian law—passed way back in the early 1900s, long before the advent of chain stores—requiring that trading stamps bear the name of the individual store that handed them out. The purpose of the law was, of course, to keep the customer informed as to who was responsible for the stamps' redemption.

I promptly sent John Heim, a boyhood friend and probably the most knowledgeable trading-stamp lawyer in America, to Canada. John was by that time my corporate counsel and eventually supervised a legal team of seven. In Canada he met with various high-level officials and came up with a simple solution to the problem. With the Canadian government's approval, stamp companies could print only the name of the chain responsible for the stamps, not each of the chain's individual stores. As a result, millions of Gold Bond stamps were subsequently issued to Canadian housewives.

By 1960 we had also fought our bloodiest battles with the anti-stamp lobby here in the United States. Despite their overwhelming popularity in the marketplace, stamps were still being hotly contested by a coalition of recalcitrant retail associations, certain supermarket chains, oil companies, and other stampless opponents, who charged that stamp programs constituted a detriment to fair trade. Stamps had been outlawed in Kansas and the District of Columbia, more than two-dozen other states had similar prohibitions under legislative consideration, and even Congress was looking into their "legality." The stamp companies were being threatened because the houswife's love affair with their gift programs was so intense. Non-stamp merchants were turning to their Congressmen to pass anti-stamp legislation.

The stamp companies fought back, of course. In North Dakota, for instance, we mounted a grassroots campaign that resulted, first, in a stamp referendum on the statewide ballot and, second, an overwhelming vote on behalf of stamps. In Washington, D.C., I went to see Hubert Humphrey, who at that time was not only one of Minnesota's Senators, but also chairman of the Senate Committee on Small Business. Humphrey, it turned out, was both sympathetic and eager to help. An erstwhile druggist back home, he had given out Gold Bond stamps himself and understood their popularity with merchants and consumers alike. The Happy Warrior joined the Great Trading Stamp War firmly on the side of stamps.

Thanks in large part to Humphrey's efforts, national anti-stamp legislation never materialized, and the anti-stamp hysteria lost much of its steam. The Senator himself remained a close personal friend and trusted ally until his death in 1978.

YET DESPITE ALL THE FUN and excitement, despite all the growth and gains, by the early 1960s there was a good, sound reason for me to be concerned about my company's future.

The trading stamp, by that time, had taken over the marketplace like no other promotional device before or since. Even stamps' most vociferous opponents acknowledged that the popularity of those little squares of paper was astonishing. More than eighty percent of the nation's grocery shoppers saved stamps, and, to meet that demand, the number of American stamp companies had soared from only four when Gold Bond began in 1938 to more than four-hundred in 1958. By that time, nineteen of the country's twenty largest supermarket chains, as well as every second gas station and a majority of the nation's drugstores, gave away stamps. Stamps, it seemed, were everywhere—and that, eventually, was the crux of the problem.

When virtually every supermarket, drugstore, and filling station in town gives some brand of stamp to its customers, no one enjoys a competitive advantage. What's more, of course, there is virtually nobody left for a company like Gold Bond to sell stamp programs to; the market, like a sponge, has become saturated.

Gold Bond's business, I hasten to point out, had not begun to fall off. On the contrary, our volume continued to increase. As a matter of fact, our biggest and best year, 1966, was still some distance down the road. Nor had the skirmishes with the anti-stamp legion taken any of the starch or sparkle out of our forces. No, it was simply a matter of my looking ahead, beyond the next quarter, beyond even the next few years, and seeing not what I wanted to see, but what was really out there on the horizon.

What I saw when I looked out into the distance was that saturated market. We had gotten to the point where I couldn't put together a five-year budget projection that would allow us to continue our normal growth pattern. No matter how hard we worked or how many ingenious promotions we mounted, the market simply wouldn't accommodate our ambitions.

I recall my father once telling me, "I'm not going to leave you a lot of money, but I'm going to leave you something better. All of America will be your territory, whatever you want to sell."

Well, in 1960 "all of America" was out there all right, but now I had to think of something new to "sell" across that vast and populous expanse. I was not about to abandon stamps, which, as I say, was still a robust business, but I did understand that the time had come to diversify.

For a while, I suppose, I was uncomfortable with the prospect. My "one good idea," after all, had done wonders for me and my company over the past twenty-two years, and it was difficult to think of branching out with other, unfamiliar, perhaps untested "ideas." At the same time, my organization was like an army that, emotionally, was simply not equipped to deal with either the status quo or retreat. I knew that all we could do was go forward.

Our initial efforts by way of diversification were predictable enough. The trading stamp was nothing more, at its core, than an incentive to buy groceries, drugstore products, and gasoline from one merchant instead of another. Thus it seemed only logical that we get into such related premium-incentive areas as manufacturer's coupons. It also seemed wise (if not strictly logical in light of our existing business) to get ourselves involved in a non-service industry, with a business requiring substantial capital rather than an idea that everyone could copy. Among our other ventures, we began, accordingly, to accumulate key parcels of land in the fast-growing suburbs just west of Minneapolis with the notion of eventually developing a major industrial park.

The hotel business was *not* one of the "new" ideas on my agenda when Tom Moore Sr., a long-time acquaintance and proprietor of the venerable Radisson Hotel in downtown Minneapolis, approached me to ask a little favor.

The Radisson was a Minneapolis landmark, a home-away-from-home for visiting dignitaries and celebrities since President William Howard Taft had been the guest-of-honor at its grand opening back in 1909. I had personally been familiar with the handsome old hotel since my college days, when I used to take dates to the Radisson's lively Flame Room to dance to the big bands. In more recent years the hotel had begun to require some extensive updating and expansion. But Moore, by then in his seventies, was having difficulty raising the necessary funding. He asked me and nine other friends if we'd be willing to help him out. In exchange for guaranteeing half of the several million dollars he needed for renovation, the ten of us would collectively receive half interest in the hotel, or five percent ownership apiece.

Though I'd never dreamed of getting into the hotel business, I thought, Well, why not? Five percent wasn't that large a stake to begin with, and my partners were a good bunch of fellows that included my banker friend Carl Pohlad and the famous bandleader Guy Lombardo. Besides, a hotel was brick-and-mortar, and wasn't that one of the areas into which I was looking to expand? I told Tom that he could count me in. I didn't realize at the time how deeply I was going to become involved.

It didn't take long, however, before I began feeling like one of those "Ten Little Indians" in the Agatha Christie whodunit: One by one, my fellow Indians began dropping. The first to go was the legendary Lombardo, whose entry fee Pohlad and I were sent down to Chicago to retrieve. It seemed that Guy, who was otherwise doing handsomely, was having some temporary cash-flow problems. When his business manager suggested that the bandleader's share be covered by the rest of the hotel's partners, then paid back to us out of his eventual earnings, I told him that the partnership couldn't operate like that. Either he puts up his share or gets out, we told his manager.

Guy got out.

Then one after another, the remaining "five-percenters,"

concerned about the fiscal obligations placed on them by the arrangement, announced their willingness to sell out at cost. I was the only one who wasn't eager to get out—who was, for that matter, amenable to buying the others' shares.

I asked Tom to level with me about the hotel business. He readily admitted that it wasn't like the good old days, when all roads, literally and figuratively both, led downtown. In 1960 more and more of the metropolitan area's convention and hospitality business was being directed to the burgeoning suburban motels. Furthermore, the airlines had made it possible for business travelers to come into town, take care of their business, and leave again in a single day, thus eliminating the need to spend the night in a hotel. He spoke about earning only a five-percent profit under the best of circumstances, and assured me that a hotel would never make a fellow rich.

On the bright side, he added, however: "A big hotel like the Radisson is still where the downtown action is. As an innkeeper, you'll always know what's going on around town." It's something, he promised me, that gets in a person's blood.

Well, I bought out the other investors and found myself the half owner of a big-city hotel, with a buy-sell clause in the final agreement. But that wasn't the end of it. Within two years Tom, who had continued to manage the property, told me he wanted out completely. He was too old, he said, to run a hotel. In keeping with our arrangement, I purchased his half of the property and, just like that, became a full-fledged hotelkeeper.

Owning a hotel had not come about by any plan, nor was it ever written down on one of those "goal slips" I was accustomed to putting in my billfold. As the tag-line of the old joke goes, it simply seemed like a good idea at the time.

CHAPTER TWELVE

Innkeeping and Incentives

ON THE FACE OF IT, trading stamps and hotels would seem a peculiar, apples-and-oranges sort of mismatch—and indeed it might have been back in the early 1960s, before major league baseball teams were owned by book publishers and book publishers were subsidiaries of television networks.

But, in fact, that original Radisson Hotel, in downtown Minneapolis, was actually a comfortably fitting addition to the Gold Bond Stamp Company. We enjoyed holding meetings in its elegant old conference rooms and putting up visiting business people in its handsomely appointed guest rooms. We also got a big kick out of establishing what soon became a downtown entertainment tradition.

I'd long appreciated the combination of good music and fine dining, and at the Villa Fontana Restaurant in Mexico City I had once seen a wonderful show featuring a pair of pianists and an ensemble of strolling violinists. When I took over the Radisson, I asked a local impresario, Al Sheehan, to put together a similar production. Al advertised for musicians and received one-hundred-and-twenty applications, sixty of which he invited to audition. Of the sixty, he finally chose ten violinists, two pianists, and a bassist. Sheehan hired Cliff Brunzell to conduct the group and be its lead violinist, then recruited a handful of other musicians from the Minneapolis Symphony Orchestra. On Valentine's Day, 1963, the Radisson Hotel's Golden Strings made their glorious debut, beginning what would become the longest-running hotel-based show in North America. With its lush sounds and elegant presentation, the Golden Strings remained a trademark of that original Radisson until the building was razed in 1982 to make room for the new Radisson Plaza Hotel Minneapolis.

I did not take an active role in the hotel's day-to-day management. Instead, upon buying Tom Moore's half of the property, I hired Tom's able and energetic son, Bob, to run it while I concentrated on stamps and our overall diversification efforts. I was not a born-and-bred hotelier, and thus thought it best to leave the details to someone who was. Besides, stamps were still a very big business—certainly *our* biggest business—and still required my tightly focused attention. At the same time, however, I had no difficulty, as a dyed-in-the-wool salesman, seeing how we could expand and enhance our hotel business. I knew, for instance, that a regional salesmen's association, which put on half-a-dozen major trade shows in Minneapolis a year, was the Radisson's largest single customer. Why not develop a merchandise-exhibit complex across the street (where sufficient space happened to be available), connect the complex to the hotel by means of a climate-controlled skyway, and go after more and even bigger shows? That's precisely what we did, and when trade shows came to town, participants displayed their wares in our new Merchandise Mart, then dined, relaxed, and slept across the street in our hotel.

It was obvious, for that matter, that if I was going to make hotelkeeping a worthwhile—that is, profitable—part of the company, we would need more properties. Radisson was a well-known and highly respected name in this part of the country, but there was only one of them. Furthermore, at best we were making, as Tom Moore had predicted, only about a five-percent profit, which wasn't too skimpy in those days, but one that could surely, I felt, be improved on.

I remember telling Bob Moore one day, "We've got to think about making more money and expanding the business."

Bob replied, "Well, where do you think we should go?"

I said, "I don't know where to go—but, wherever we go, you'll have to run the show. In any case, I'd rather have you running *two* hotels than just one."

Not long after that, we broke ground on a choice piece of real estate in the booming—but, at that time, hotel-less—Minneapolis suburb of Bloomington. We made a deal with Tony Bernardi, who owned the land, to join us fifty-fifty in the project. While investigating Bernardi's background before the "marriage," we found that Tony would have an interest, his partners in Italy an interest, even the Vatican an interest. It seems that any real estate development that the Italian group invested in included a twenty-five-percent share for the Vatican. I figured that if the Pope trusted these men, so could I. The deluxe, 450-room Radisson South Hotel opened its doors in October 1970.

Earlier that year we opened another new Radisson hotel in Duluth, Minnesota. The 200-room Radisson Duluth, whose distinctive round tower looked out on the city's picturesque Lake Superior harbor, was built in cooperation with several Duluth business interests and was the first major hotel erected in that community in fifty years.

In the meantime, we had begun to buy a few other, long-established hotels around the Midwest, including the Blackstone in Omaha and the Cornhusker in Lincoln, Nebraska. The Cornhusker was particularly attractive to us because in the fall of the year people came to Lincoln from all over the state to watch their beloved University of Nebraska play football; once in town, the Big Red faithful jammed the local hotels. The big, aptly named Cornhusker, with its 400 rooms, could by itself accommodate a lot of fans during those golden autumn weekends.

I might add that over the next several years I would learn another valuable lesson—this time about the hospitality business—and I would pay through the nose for my education. The lesson was simply this: No matter what you did with an old hotel, it was still an old hotel. Those big, old hotels like the Cornhusker, despite their former glitter and glory, had become dinosaurs by the 1960s. They were destined to lose huge amounts of their business to the newer, trendier, often smaller and more efficiently run hotels and motels going up around them, both downtown and in the suburbs. While in the old days travelers were fiercely loyal to a favored hotel, in the contemporary world the business was entirely up for grabs. In most of the major U.S. markets, there were too many good facilities among which modern travelers could choose. There were, of course, exceptions to the rule. Some magnificent old hotels had been continually renovated and updated, and remained profitable. But such establishments were increasingly few and far between.

Having digested that difficult truth, I decided that from then on, glory and tradition would have to give way to a hard-headed pragmatism. Our expansion in the hospitality business would, in other words, be confined to new—or at least newer—hotels.

DURING THE EARLY 1960s, while we were receiving an education in the business of hotels, we were also diversifying and expanding into other directions.

I had gotten involved, on my own, in a series of multi-million-dollar joint ventures with my old friend and faithful duck-hunting companion Robert Naegele, head of Naegele Outdoor Advertising Company. The ventures included the joint purchase of several regional divisions of the huge General Outdoor Advertising Company. Naegele and his people managed the business on the partnership's behalf, and, for more than two decades, it was a very profitable arrangement for the both of us.

Bob and his right-hand man, Dick Condon, always found me an eager investor. One day I remarked that I was willing to invest with them not only because of their astute management ability, but because compared to my other businesses, theirs seemed remarkably trouble-free. Bob laughed. At my insistence, he admitted that he had passed the word down his chain of command that I was never to be "bothered" with news of any difficulty their far-flung operations might be facing. "Curt is having all the problems he needs in his own business," Bob told his executives. "Let's solve our problems ourselves." And, in reality, I learned, two of their operations were at that moment being manned by executives because of strikes; a third was involved in a squabble with the local newspaper, which was campaigning to do away with billboards.

But my faith in my friend never wavered. On one occasion I was out of the country when Bob called with a request for cash. My regular secretary was out to lunch when I called in for messages. Her replacement, looking at the message slip, could tell me only that "Bob Naegele called and wants $2 million." When I asked her what he needed it for, she said she couldn't say. "All I know," she added, looking at the slip, "is that he needs it today."

Obviously, I had to make a quick decision. Relying on

Leatha and Charles Carlson,
my mother and father,
in about 1905.

Little snowman. Yours truly,
at the age of three.

I've always enjoyed a good party—and being in the driver's seat.
With siblings and playmates at the age of five.

Onward and upward.
Graduating from West High School
in Minneapolis, 1932.

Licensed to sell. In 1938 the Gold Bond Stamp Company
was officially pronounced a Minnesota corporation.

Good as gold.
An early Gold Bond saver's book.

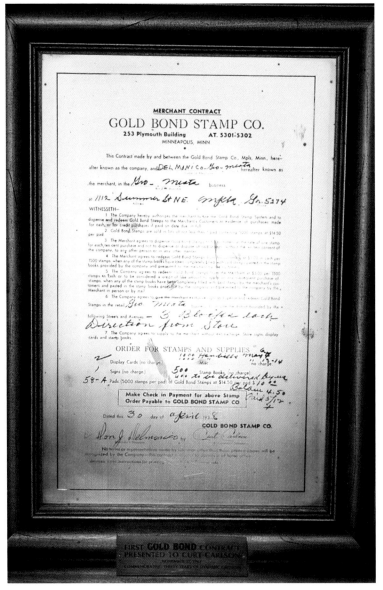

One of Gold Bond's first contracts was with Delmonico's,
a northeast Minneapolis grocery store. More than fifty years later,
Delmonico's still gives Gold Bond stamps with purchases.

Stepping out.
Arleen and I and our beautiful daughters,
Marilyn (left) and Barbara, circa 1945.

Honoring our mother and father
at their golden wedding anniversary in 1956.
Standing, from left to right: Warren and Jane Carlson,
Dean and Elaine Carlson, yours truly and Arleen,
Aileen (Carlson) Miller and Dwight Miller,
and Hazel and Ken Carlson.

Beginning in 1953, Gold Bond savers could redeem their stamps
for top-quality premiums at our first gift center,
on Nicollet Avenue in downtown Minneapolis.

On horseback at the Zuhrah Shrine Showdeo in 1955.

Gold Bond's Mr. Inside, Joe Hunt,
reviews our building plans, circa 1960.

Thrifty Scotsman Sandy Saver
helped me break ground for our Plymouth, Minnesota,
headquarters in 1961.

Opened in 1962, the sleek, sprawling Plymouth facility served
as world headquarters for more than 25 years.

The Gold Bond creed has been stated and restated countless times.
It's even been rendered in needlepoint—by Jean Stagg,
wife of Gold Bond executive Charles Stagg.

A casual moment with Arleen
in 1963, our twenty-fifth year of marriage.

Our thirty-fifth year in business
was a gala family affair,
where proud parents and grandparents
celebrated with the kids.

CURTIS L. CARLSON

PRESIDENT AND CHAIR-
MAN OF THE BOARD
OF THE CARLSON
COMPANIES, IS THE
RECIPIENT OF THE
1976, NEWSPAPER-
BOYS' HALL OF FAME
AWARD.

AS A BOY HE DELIVERED
THE MINNEAPOLIS JOURNAL
IN 1925.

MR. CARLSON WAS EDUCATED
AT LAKE HARRIET/EDINA
ELEMENTARY WEST HIGH
SCHOOL, MINNEAPOLIS, AND
THE UNIVERSITY OF MINNESOTA,
BA/ECONOMICS, 1937.

IN 1938, AFTER A SHORT STAY
WITH PROCTOR & GAMBLE
UPON GRADUATING FROM THE
UNIVERSITY OF MINNESOTA,
HE DECIDED TO GO INTO
BUSINESS FOR HIMSELF.
IT WAS THEN HE LAUNCHED
THE GOLD BOND STAMP PRO-
GRAM WHICH WAS TO GROW
TO ANNUAL COMBINED SALES
OF MORE THAN $400 MILLION.

HE PRESENTLY HOLDS OFFICES
IN MANY COMPANIES.
HE MARRIED ARLEEN MARTIN
OF MINNEAPOLIS, MINNESOTA
ON JUNE 30, 1938 — TWO CHILDREN,
MARILYN (MRS. GLEN NELSON),
AND BARBARA (MRS. EDWIN GAGE III).
HIS FAVORITE HOBBIES:
PHOTOGRAPHY AND HORSES.

HILBERT BUSHEY

In 1976—more than fifty years
after I took on my first paper route—I was named
to the Newspaper-Boys' Hall of Fame.

Wearing the Royal Order of the North Star, Commander,
presented in 1976 by Sweden's king,
His Majesty Carl XVI Gustaf.

Another new hotel is opened
with the help of legendary explorer
and namesake Pierre Radisson.

Our first billion-dollar goal
was reiterated in 1974. Four years later,
it was mission accomplished.

The E.F. MacDonald incentive and motivation firm
became part of Carlson Companies in 1981.
Here, Harry Greenough (left) and Skip Gage (right)
join hands with MacDonald chairman George C. Gilfillen Jr.
and me to mark the happy occasion.

With Marcus Wallenberg, one of Sweden's
leading industrialists, at a 1981 Swedish Council
of America dinner in the Twin Cities.

Receiving the Linnean Medal
of the Royal Swedish Academy of Sciences
from King Carl Gustaf in 1982.

At the 1982 grand opening
of the Radisson hotel in Raleigh,
North Carolina.

The incomparable Golden Strings were a
downtown Minneapolis tradition at the Flame Room
in the original Radisson Hotel.

Arleen and I were pleased to greet
former President Jimmy Carter when he spoke
as a Distinguished Carlson Lecturer
at the University of Minnesota in 1984.

New Hampshire College
in Manchester named me an Honorary
Doctor of Humane Letters in 1985.

Who would have thought it possible?
Soviet Communist leader Mikhail Gorbachev
talked trade with the capitalists in Minneapolis
during his historic 1990 visit.

Sweden's ambassador to the United States, Anders Thunborg,
helped dedicate Carl Milles' soaring *Man and His Genius*
at our new World Headquarters
in Minnetonka, Minnesota, in 1990.

All smiles. Business and friendship
go hand-in-hand as Moscow Mayor Yuri Luzhkov
joins my daughter Marilyn and me
during a recent Minnesota trip.

With Governor Arne Carlson (left)
and University of Minnesota president Nils Hasselmo
at the dedication of the Carlson Travel, Tourism, and Hospitality
Chair at the U of M in Minneapolis.

Sweden's far-flung sons and daughters
are watched with interest by the news media in Sweden.
Here's a sampling of the press attention we've received there
over the past several years.

Carlson Companies and its people
have rarely shrunk from publicity at home or abroad.
Magazine and newspaper coverage
from around the world.

Relaxed and reflective.

Fifty-one years after launching the Gold Bond
Stamp Company from a rented apartment, we opened the twin
towers of our grand, new World Headquarters in 1989.

We'll break ground for the $45-million
Carlson School of Management building in 1995. Designed
by Ellerbe Beckett, the facility will be ready in 1997.

In 1994 our Carlson Travel Group and Paris-based
Wagonlit Travel united to form Carlson Wagonlit Travel,
a worldwide business-travel management venture backed by a
network of more than four-thousand locations in one-hundred-and-
twenty-five countries. Marking the occasion during ceremonies in
the French capital are (seated, left to right) Paul Dubrule,
co-chairman of the Accor Group, parent company of Wagonlit
Travel; Curt Carlson; Marilyn Nelson, vice-chair of Carlson
Holdings and co-chair of Carlson Wagonlit Travel; Gérard Pelisson,
co-chairman of the Accor Group; (standing) Hervé Gourio,
co-president and chief executive officer of Carlson Wagonlit Travel;
Christian Pierret, general director of the Accor Group; Travis
Tanner, president of Carlson Travel Group and co-president and
chief executive officer of Carlson Wagonlit Travel; and Jean-Marc
Simon, the Accor Group's senior executive vice president and
co-chair of Carlson Wagonlit Travel.

The board of Carlson Holdings, Inc., in 1994. Seated,
left to right: Marilyn Nelson, Curt Carlson, and Barbara Gage.
Standing: Matthew Levitt (special advisor to the board),
Dr. Glen Nelson, Arleen Carlson, and Skip Gage.

Eighty violinists from the Wayzata Elementary Strings in our
west-suburban "neighborhood" dropped by to serenade employees
and guests at my eightieth birthday party July 7, 1994.

All in the family. My grandson Curtis Nelson,
president of our Country Hospitality Corporation,
joins his mother Marilyn and me
in this portrait of three generations
of Carlson Companies leadership.

my confidence in Bob and the exhaustive research he and his staff put behind the company's investments, I told the woman, "O.K., give it to him." I was sure I wouldn't be burned—and, as things turned out, I wasn't.

As a company, meanwhile, we had branched out along more familiar roads in the ever-widening world of premium incentives. "We are expanding and enlarging into related premium fields," I told my staff at the time. "We're the people-motivating people," I reminded them, "—motivating people to buy."

In 1963, reflecting our expansion in the premium business, we changed our corporate name. The "Gold Bond Stamp Company," with its single-product denotation, became the "Premium Service Corporation," which emphasized its broader-based premium orientation. Under the PSC umbrella were gathered a handful of our more recently created divisions, including the Performance Incentives Corporation, the Premium Corporation of America, and Premium Distributors, Inc. The names themselves left little doubt, either within or outside of the parent company, about the general nature of our business.

Performance Incentives Corporation (PIC) had been formed in 1960, in a partnership with Grand Union, a New Jersey-based supermarket chain that owned Triple S trading stamps. The new company, which focused on employee motivation, was initially headquartered in Hackensack, where it could serve the big East Coast markets, and operated by Triple S president William Preis. Such major American corporations as Goodyear, Autolite, and New York Savings Bank were among its early clients.

Here in Minneapolis we'd launched a division called Communications Associates to help corporations develop fresh sales-stimulating concepts. As Harry Greenough, who headed the new division, stated it, "People are moved by ideas, and ideas are the business of Communications Associates. When you're a company fighting giants like E.F. MacDonald and J. Walter Thompson, your ideas have to be giant-killers or you don't survive." With those words, of course, Harry could well have been summing up our entire corporate mentality since Day One some twenty-five years earlier. Under the new PSC umbrella, Communications Associates became part of our Premium Corporation of America division.

Our critical operating principal was based on the conviction I'd carried with me since my days with Procter & Gamble—that as behavioral or performance incentives, gifts were far more valuable than money to the recipient. The gifts that Performance Incentives Corporation suggested for its clients were, however, anything but conventional: half-a-million Gold Bond Stamps, for instance, or an all-expense-paid trip to Paris. The best news was the gifts worked very effectively for our clients, who quickly included such large and prestigious corporations as Honeywell, 3M, and Hormel.

Still another division, Premium Distributors, Inc., was more directly connected with our original incentive, the trading stamp. PDI supplied a good-sized roster of outside stamp companies with premiums and, in some cases, published their catalogs.

My personal interest in manufacturer's coupons predated all of those businesses and divisions. Again, the idea wasn't a new one; it dated back well into the nineteenth century. Two large, locally based food companies, General Mills and Pillsbury, had long used, respectively, their Betty Crocker Coupons and Thrift Stars. The fact that these companies continued their incentive programs (renewable for free tableware) for so many years was proof of their continuing appeal. The logic of such coupons sounded reasonable enough. If stamps could draw customers to a supermarket, why couldn't coupons—likewise redeemable for gifts— draw customers to an individual product? If stamps could encourage customer loyalty to a particular store, why couldn't coupons encourage customer loyalty to a particular brand of cake mix?

During the mid-1950s—with the cooperation of a local Super Valu store-owner, Bob Tait, and the subrosa assistance of my secretary, Dee Kemnitz—I began my own quiet market research. Dee and I would fill little glassine envelopes with twenty-five Gold Bond Stamps (redeemable, of course, for premiums) and attach those envelopes to selected products on Bob Tait's shelves; Bob would then keep track of the sales of those products. What I discovered in the course of that research reinforced my long-held hunch: manufacturer's coupons, with the proper application, could indeed work wonders. They could add to the lead of a top-selling product or boost the competitive position of an also-ran.

My idea was to develop a broad-based venture with all the manufacturers that were then using coupons. A new common coupon, perhaps used in conjunction with stamps and redeemable for both cash and gifts, could then reach dozens of potent markets. The only problem seemed to be the technology—rather, the *lack* of it. There was simply no device at that time that could effectively and efficiently sort and count the great quantities of redeemed coupons such a program would generate. For want of such a device—and because of the Safeway opportunity that presented itself at that point in the company's history—I put the manufacturer's coupon idea on the back-burner.

But technical problems and other distractions notwithstanding, I never forgot about the possibility of those coupons. As a matter of fact, I can recall, sometime during the late '50s, looking down at the twinkling lights of a large city from the window of an airliner. "Just think," I said to Harry Greenough, who was sitting beside me. "All those people down there, and we aren't doing any business with them." My goal was to do business with every last man and woman in America, and coupons would be an ideal means by which to do it.

Still, it was not until 1961 that my airborne rumination became a reality. Honeywell had developed an electronic device called an Orthoscanner that would allow us to sort and count coupons, with nearly total accuracy, at the rate of fifteen-hundred a minute. At last, the technology had caught up to us. We quickly established a new company to distribute a new coupon called Gift Stars—and, before long, we had a stellar list of subscribers that included Hills Bros. coffee, Kleenex tissues, Mennen baby-care products, Oscar Meyer meats, Old Gold cigarettes, Vaseline hair tonic, and Alcoa aluminum-foil wrap. And, when Gift Stars were test-marketed with these products and others in 1963, we mounted the kind of promotional blitz that until then we'd reserved for our biggest Gold Bond promotions.

The coupons were an immediate hit. During our initial tests in Denver and Salt Lake City, the sale of packaged coffee bearing Gift Stars jumped one-hundred percent, the sale of packaged meats even higher. Spectacular increases were reported for Gift Star-bearing products as diverse as macaroni and soft drinks. After a second test, in St. Louis, yielded similar results, no fewer than two-hundred-sixty-three additional manufacturers signed up for our program.

The next year we bought Premium Associates, the company that owned Red Scissors coupons, and turned that money-losing operation around. Later, when Gift Stars expanded into Red Scissors' traditional territory in the Deep South, we sold Premium Associates for a tidy profit.

As our coupon business developed across the country, no single group of manufacturers made bigger or better use of coupons than the big cigarette makers. P. Lorillard, which manufactured Old Golds, was the first big tobacco company to subscribe to the Gift Stars program. Coupons on packs of participating Lorillard brands were each worth five points, which was equal to five trading stamps. The coupons, however, could be redeemed in three ways: for cash, for merchandise, or in combination with trading stamps.

Not surprisingly, the coupons were enormously popular among both smokers and the tobacco companies. Lorillard, with exclusive cigarette-industry rights to Gift Stars, decided to carry the coupons on all of its brands, and at one point ordered a single printing of 172-million coupons. When Liggett & Meyers wanted to use a similar program to revive interest in its flagging Chesterfield brand, we created a new entry called LMC, for Luxury Merchandise Coupons, in a move that reminded some of our company's old-timers of our Top Value venture with Kroger a decade earlier.

By the middle 1960s, several billion Gift Star and LMC coupons were in active circulation, and some $50-million worth of merchandise was distributed annually as coupon premiums. Our Gift Stars and Gold Bond gift catalogs were pored over by twice the number of people who "read" the Sears Roebuck and Montgomery Ward catalogs put together!

A T ABOUT THE SAME TIME we were moving, as a company, so energetically into other areas of endeavor, we were also moving, as a staff, into other areas of town. In 1962, after more than a decade on Hennepin Avenue in downtown Minneapolis, we moved ourselves lock, stock, and barrel into a brand-new, 80,000-square-foot world headquarters office building and 110,000-square-foot warehouse on the site of an industrial park we were beginning to develop in the northwestern suburb of Plymouth.

I had already begun thinking about building a retreat even farther removed from the bustle of the big city. The retreat, as I envisioned it, would function as both a brainstorming center for our various divisions and a rest-and-relaxation hideaway for my staff. It would also provide an isolated vacation and special-occasion site for my family. Keeping the retreat idea close to the vest, I instructed Ann Richardson, my secretary, to look around for an architect. Ann was well-suited for the assignment. The daughter of an Ohio construction-company owner, she'd been reading blueprints since she was a little girl. After college she joined the engineering department of a small manufacturer, and later, as my right-hand assistant, she accepted the responsibility of overseeing the building of our new home office.

Lake Minnesuing, in northwestern Wisconsin, was likewise appropriate to my secret retreat plans. When I was a kid, my siblings and I had spent many wonderful summer days literally in the middle of that lake—on and around an island then owned in part by my Uncle George. It was situated in a beautiful part of the country, deep in a pristine part of the North Woods favored by such serious fishermen as Calvin Coolidge, and I had grown over the years to consider it an important part of me. Lake Minnesuing, in fact, I considered to be my very own. Some years earlier I had purchased from my parents their summer cottage on the lake. I knew the lake well and knew the additional property I wanted to buy.

I eventually purchased, for $14,000, a good-sized farm property that fronted the lake and overlooked the island of my boyhood vacations. Ann then selected an architect named Herb Bloomberg, who visited the site with us one cold December day and then went to work enhancing the rough sketch I had given him. Within a few weeks, construction began on what would eventually become my million-dollar dream project. And, believe it or not, the project was kept a secret throughout the period of construction. Among my family and staff, only Ann and Joe Hunt (who signed the construction checks) knew what was going on up there in the Wisconsin woods.

When the Minnesuing Acres Lodge was completed in 1961, my family, my staff, and I were all absolutely delighted. The style could be described as "sophisticated rustic" and featured a board-and-batten exterior, hand-shake roof, and plenty of exposed beams inside. Special hardwoods for the construction had been brought in from such distant points as California and North Carolina. The lodge was large enough to sleep seventy persons, and different parts of the complex were connected by a maze of halls and tunnels. In addition to the living quarters, there was an auditorium, a game room and bowling alley, and an indoor swimming pool fed by a miniature waterfall. Elsewhere on the grounds was a stable for our riding horses, a nine-hole "pitch-'n'-putt" golf course, and facilities for tennis, archery, and trapshooting.

There was an interesting sidelight to the project as well. Herb Bloomberg was bidding on the new Hazeltine Golf Course club house being planned just west of Minneapolis. The owner of the place was Pudge Hefflefinger, the former All-American football player at Yale and erstwhile chairman of the Peavey Company, one of America's foremost millers. Bloomberg had learned, it seems, that he was not going to get the Hazeltine job, so, in a last-ditch effort to turn things in his direction, he prevailed upon Hefflefinger to fly up to Minnesuing Acres to see the lodge he was building for me. Hefflefinger walked into the lodge—where only the Great Hall had been finished—and exclaimed, "Herb, this is exactly what I'm looking for. You've got the job!"

But that wasn't all. Robert Trent Jones, the renowned golf-course designer who was working on the Hazeltine links at the time, had come along with Hefflefinger and Bloomberg for the ride. Making the most of the opportunity, Herb asked Jones for some advice on the construction of my little nine-hole course, and Jones generously provided it. In fact, Jones stayed on after Hefflefinger returned to the Twin Cities and instructed Bloomberg and a dozen workmen in the fine art of golf-course building. When he finally departed three days later, all that remained to do was put down the sod.

I presume that my little par-three course is the only one in America planned and installed by Robert Trent Jones— for free!

CHAPTER THIRTEEN

Sailing Forward, Fighting Back

IHAD LONG BELIEVED that buying a man's time for eight hours a day was one thing, but that capturing his heart and mind for the longer haul was something else altogether. That belief was the cornerstone of so many of the employee-incentive programs our Performance Incentives Corporation was selling in the 1960s. It was also at the center of our own corporate incentive program, in which exceptional performance—the kind of performance I demanded of my employees—was encouraged and acknowledged with exceptional rewards.

That long-ago Procter & Gamble wristwatch never far from my mind, I insisted that my company's outstanding performers were not only paid an appropriate salary, but honored with more distinctively tangible rewards as well. Each of my top executives was given, for instance, a new Cadillac or other luxury automobile every year. (A line of those handsome cars, parked side by side and all painted the company's trademark gold, was for many years a familiar sight at our world headquarters.) The wives of our biggest producers received gorgeous fur coats, and husbands and wives together were treated to all-expense-paid company trips to exciting ports-of-call in the Caribbean, Latin America, Scandinavia, continental Europe, and the Orient.

Spouses, I discovered early, were essential to our managers' success and, therefore, essential to the success of the company. I spoke earlier about the critical importance of a supportive spouse to a fledgling entrepreneur. Let me now say a few words about the critical importance of supportive spouses to that entrepreneur's employees.

I have learned, among my many lessons, that happy family men and women make the best workers, be they upper-echelon executives or mail clerks. They tend to be more serious about their jobs, more responsible in their duties, and, because they have more than just themselves to support, generally harder-working than their unmarried counterparts. They tend to be hungrier, because they are working for their children at home and for their children's future as well as for their own. They seem to be more stable, too, and stability is extremely important. The most brilliant individuals in the world aren't going to do you much good if they're unable to keep their minds on their tasks, or if they're constantly jumping from one job to another. I would much rather go with employees who have set career objectives for themselves and steadily progress toward their goals, always placing service to their customers first. In my experience, happily married men and women are much more likely to give you steady, productive performance.

At the same time, a significant problem for any company is a happily married person whose spouse wants to live or work elsewhere. Though most of our workforce here at headquarters hails from Minnesota, we recruit a fair number of key people from other parts of the country. We've learned that it pays to interview both such prospective transplants *and* their spouses before hiring. If the candidate and the spouse would be coming from, say, California or Florida, we not only talk about the high quality of life here in Minnesota, we level with them about our cold, snowy winters, and urge them both to speak up if the climate (or any other potentially negative aspect of our part of the country) would be a problem. We simply know from long experience that no matter how much a person may like the job, if his or her spouse is unhappy under the new arrangement, the person is not likely to be with us for very long.

We've learned this, too: Get a salesperson's spouse involved in the company's goals, and that salesperson is going to work all the harder to help achieve those goals. It's a little like having a lot of extra sales managers on your staff—motivating, encouraging, reminding the individual salesperson of the reward waiting at the end of all the extra effort.

For many years, we've invited spouses to our big annual meeting where we announce the company's sales quotas and achievement awards. We've also worked hard to generate a lot of enthusiasm about the company-paid trips that take our top performers and their spouses on "once-in-a-lifetime" kinds of trips. The winners, I can assure you, never forget those prizes, or why they were awarded to them, and neither do their spouses. For the people who receive them, those trips are a source not only of spectacular memories, but of great and lasting pride.

I won't pretend, though, that all of our trips have been unqualified successes. I am reminded, for example, of the ill-starred voyage of the good ship Funchal, which carried one-hundred-thirty of our executives and award-winners and their spouses on a gala twenty-fifth anniversary cruise in 1963. After a tiring Minnesota-to-Portugal air and land journey complicated by nasty weather, we boarded the Funchal in Lisbon and set out on what we all expected to be a fabulous Atlantic cruise to the Canary Islands.

Once out of port, however, the dream vacation turned into something that resembled a nightmare. The ship tossed and rolled unmercifully on the heavy seas. Ann Richardson, who had arranged the trip, reported having to shower with one arm hooked around a water pipe lest she be hurled out of the shower stall, and then having to get dressed while hunkered down on her hands and knees. In the ship's lounge, meanwhile, those few hardy souls who had ventured out of their cabins were fast going green in the face from the relentless tipsy-turvy motion.

The night was awful as the Funchal plied the churning deep. First thing the next morning Elliot Srebrenick, one of our top salesmen from Arizona, begged Ann to have him and his wife put ashore at Madeira, where they could spend the rest of the trip on terra firma. "Please, Ann," said poor Elliot. "We'll do *anything*. We'll even pay our own hotel bill!"

Ann, however, insisted that the Srebrenicks stay aboard. Things would get better, she promised him. And besides, she pointed out, there were business meetings to attend.

Well, things did *not* get a whole lot better, and the meetings, at which I presided, were poorly attended as many of even our stoutest hearts chose to lie low in their bunks.

And at the cruise's end, it was Elliot Srebrenick who had the last—or, at least, the most memorable—word on the subject.

"This trip," he muttered upon docking back in Lisbon, "should have been for the losers."

A NOTHER TRIP stands prominently in my mind for another, more sobering reason. That departure, in the fall of 1964, coincided with the arrival of totally unexpected bad news—that the Safeway Foods division in Phoenix was discontinuing its Gold Bond stamp program the following year. There was no explanation—simply the bad news in the form of a registered letter. And it came just a day or two before our scheduled cruise to Montego Bay in Jamaica.

As you might expect, we were stunned. Our Southwest territorial manager at the time, Glen Johnson, took the news especially hard. Glen, in fact, told his wife that in light of the startling reversal down in Phoenix, the two of them wouldn't be going along on the company's Caribbean outing.

But when I heard about Glen's intention to abandon the trip, I called him in and told him neither to despair nor to cancel his travel plans. I pointed out that Phoenix would be there when he got back. "This will be an historic trip," I told him, "and I want you to go along and enjoy yourself. Then I want you to get down there to Arizona and work your tail off." All of which he did. He and his wife went along on that trip and enjoyed themselves. Then Glen went down to Phoenix and worked like crazy to recoup our lost business.

Safeway, it turned out, had dropped the use of stamps for the increasingly popular practice of store-wide discounting. Furthermore, as Glen discovered, the chain's decision was final. But Safeway wasn't the only big game in town. Even bigger was the Bayless chain, which boasted almost twice as many supermarkets in Arizona. The problem was, Bayless (and all the other major chains in the area) had by that time gotten deeply involved in other stamp programs. Bayless, in fact, owned Frontier Stamps in partnership with Furr's Markets of Texas. Well, we decided that if we wanted to do business with Bayless, we'd simply have to buy its stake in Frontier Stamps, which we did—and, in the process, guaranteed the big chain a ten-percent increase in business.

As it happened, the loss of Safeway in Arizona was more than offset by the acquisition of Frontier. And when the

Safeway in El Paso dropped Gold Bond a short time later, we bought out Furr's share in Frontier and by that means kept our hand in the south and west Texas markets as well.

But while we were winning those individual skirmishes, we were gradually beginning to lose the war. Nineteen-sixty-six was Gold Bond Stamps' biggest year, with sales of $200 million; the following year, however, stamp sales declined by a million pads. Despite our best, intensified promotional efforts, despite working ourselves into such new niches of the market as banks and savings-and-loan associations, despite my own unflagging belief in the continuing power of stamps—despite it all, the popularity of stamps continued to wane. All over the country the big supermarket chains were abandoning the little square pieces of paper that had, only a decade before, revolutionized the way they sold groceries.

We did not lie down to die, mind you. We recouped whatever lost business we could and continued to add new accounts, and we actually recorded some slight gains in our total number of accounts. But we were well aware of the declining trend line for stamps, and, as we struggled to keep Gold Bond strong and vibrant, we continued to chart a course of prudent diversification.

In 1968, for instance, we bought out the other half of Performance Incentives Corporation from Grand Union, moved its operation center to the Twin Cities, and merged it with a small locally based motivational firm named Robinson-Seidl, which we had acquired more recently. We also launched a new division, Mail Marketing, to develop direct-mail promotions that would take advantage of the public's growing interest in credit cards.

I told my staff at the time that the key word had become "synergism." That means, I told them, that there were now a number of different facets to our company and that the total value of those facets would be greater than the sum of their individual parts. Synergism would become a concept, indeed, that grew in importance and remains, some twenty-five years later, absolutely central to the operation of our business.

I also made it perfectly clear to everyone on board at the time that we needed to be flexible, that we needed to be willing and able to adapt to the opportunities of a new era. No matter how large and profitable our organization had become on the strength of the trading stamp, we could no longer depend on the stamp business alone for any substantial future growth. I told my people that it might be difficult for some of them, having been dedicated to trading stamps for decades, to now devote their hearts and minds to other ideas; God knows, I assured them, I could understand what they were feeling. But it simply had to be done. A company, like any other living organism, must not only grow, it must be able to adapt to its changing environment if it wishes to survive and prosper. So, of course, must the people who run it.

It was important to keep in mind at that time that we were never, strictly speaking, in merely the stamp business. We had always been in the *motivational* business. Thus, if trading stamps were no longer the best means by which to motivate people, we would energetically and enthusiastically find other, even better ways to do the job. And that, of course, is what we did—with manufacturer's coupons, corporate incentive programs, and our various other products and services of the time. Particulars aside, it was—and is—the way an entrepreneur must carry on when the time comes for his "one good idea" to give way to another.

People say that I'm a sentimental fellow—and, in many

settings, I suppose I am. But when it comes to making the hard choices in business, I have always tried to set sentiment and emotion to the side, and, after a dry-eyed analysis of the situation, act in the way I believed to be best for the business.

To the extent that it means clinging to the "good old days" and outmoded ways of doing business, I believe that sentiment can be fatal to an entrepreneur. In times of opportunity and change, sentiment must yield to flexibility and pragmatism, or those "good old days" will blind him to the future.

D URING THE MID- AND LATE 1960s, it had come down to the survival of the fittest in the trading-stamp business. Dozens of stamp companies, lacking the will or the wherewithal to adapt to the times, withered and died. Happily, the Gold Bond Stamp Company carried on as the Premium Service Corporation. PSC not only "carried on," I should add, but continued to develop as a dynamic, multifaceted, growth-oriented organization.

Stamps were still the largest single part of the business, but our diversification was demanding a new kind of corporate structure that reflected the fact that the company was no longer a one-product company—or, for that matter, a one-man band. Accordingly, I hired the respected management-consulting firm of Booz, Allen & Hamilton to come in, analyze our systems and operations, and recommend ways to restructure the operation. The result was a contemporary organization that separated trading stamps and coupons into two discrete operating units, with Glen Johnson promoted to national sales manager for Gold Bond and Harry Greenough in charge of the coupons (and our other non-stamp-based incentive plans). My old friend (and former

Federal Trade Commission lawyer) John Heim was named vice president of our expanded and increasingly important legal department. Kurt Retzler became vice president and controller, in charge of our similarly expanded and important accounting section. Richard E. Karkow joined us as director of finance to help mastermind our increasingly leveraged expansion. Ann Richardson, my erstwhile secretary and co-conspirator in the Great Minnesuing Acres Adventure, became administrative assistant with the rank of V.P.

At that time we also decided to change our corporate name again. The consultants argued that a new name would better reflect our growing diversity. I myself believed that, in addition, there was always a certain no-nonsense credibility in a fellow's putting his own name on his business. I figured that no matter what field we might be dealing in, the people we were dealing with would like to know the name of the individual on whose desk the buck finally stopped.

So it was that our various and increasingly diversified operations became officially known in 1973 as "Carlson Companies, Inc."

Uncharted Waters

THE REORGANIZATION of what had become, by the middle 1970s, Carlson Companies, Inc., enabled me not only to take a longer look at the future, but also to make a broader assessment of the wide world of opportunity that lay all around us. Though Gold Bond stamps were still our dominant product, they were no longer our only one, and once having expanded beyond that initial "idea," I was free to consider all kinds of alternatives and additions.

Over the course of the previous few years, we had purchased about twenty smaller stamp companies, including the aforementioned Frontier operation in Arizona and Texas. But beyond stamps—beyond, for that matter, coupons and other premium-based products and services—there waited plenty of other possibilities. We had already diversified into hotels, of course, but now even more disparate fields of endeavor lay open to us.

I was not intent on building an empire simply for the sake of building an empire. Some of my executives and associates may have found me, at times, imperious, but I can assure you that I had no overwhelming desire to be an emperor. I simply, as I've said before, believed in the absolute necessity of growth. I believed in growth when I was first getting started and was struggling for new accounts. I believed in growth when I bought out Truman Johnson's half of the company in order to expand nationwide. I believed in growth when we began to diversify and broaden the sweep of our operations. I believe in growth today, after more than fifty years in business. The alternative to growth, I believe, is an inevitable retrogression and decline.

At the same time, though I'm willing to make mistakes, I don't consider myself a fool. There's an old Danish proverb that I like: "Don't sail out farther than you can row back." Applied to our early diversification, that philosophy might well have helped keep us out of treacherous waters. I'm not saying that all of our acquisitions during that period proved to be either wise or successful. What I'm saying is that, eager as we were to add to our tonnage, we never risked the whole boat for the sake of additional cargo. Nor did we ever sail out so far that we couldn't, if worst came to worst, make our way back to shore. Put in a somewhat dryer manner, we took risks, because taking risks is how an entrepreneurial company grows; but we did not—as a mature and experienced entrepreneurial company—risk more than we could afford to lose in a worst-case situation. To have done so, in my opinion, wouldn't have been heroic—it would have been reckless.

We did not, as far as that goes, believe in what has been widely described and hotly debated as "hostile" takeovers. While we were aggressive and admittedly opportunistic in our acquisition efforts, we had no desire to grow by force or through any cut-throat maneuvering and bitter confrontation. Before we made an overture to another company, we first assured ourselves, with the assistance of reliable third-party sources, that the company would be congenial to an outside suitor. If the company was not amenable to discussion—or if its financial situation, given a closer look, made our attention inappropriate—we simply went elsewhere.

Once we'd decided to expand through acquisition, we were willing to explore a lot of widely varying possibilities— some of them entirely foreign to the kinds of businesses with which we were familiar. Our criteria were relatively simple. Generally speaking, we figured that if we acquired a company that operated in a field where we were already doing business (stamps would be an obvious example), we would run it with our own proven and experienced people, and expect to recoup our investment in five years. If we didn't know the field, we would try to ride with the acquired company's existing management, and, because of the heightened risk inherent in such a plan, expect to get our money back in *three* years. If we determined that the five- or three-year deadline would be impossible to meet, we didn't make the deal.

I can recall many occasions when my top-level executives and I would be bouncing around the names of certain other companies. Somebody would get excited about this or that company as a possible acquisition, and I would say, "All right, that sounds good. But do we get our money back in five years?" If the fellow said, "No, but we could get it back in five-and-a-half," I would reply, "Nope, that isn't good enough. Five is the limit."

We have, in more recent years, adopted a considerably more restrictive set of acquisition criteria, which I will describe later in this chapter. At the time, however, if we were not quite willing to plumb the more treacherous depths of the sea, we were downright eager to explore some interesting uncharted waters.

WE HAD BEEN IN THE HOTEL BUSINESS, you will recall, since 1962, when I bought the original Radisson in downtown Minneapolis. Since then, our innkeeping activity had been expanding in fits and starts, with the purchase of existing properties in Omaha, Lincoln, Wichita, and Denver, and with the construction of the Radisson South in suburban Minneapolis and the Radisson Duluth in northern Minnesota.

Tom Moore had been right—innkeeping could indeed work its way into a fellow's blood. Aside from the corporate conveniences of our owning those hotels, I personally enjoyed being at the heart of the downtown action, meeting a lot of interesting and important people, and listening with a proprietary ear to the beautiful sounds of the Flame Room's Golden Strings violin show. But for all of that enjoyment we were not making money; as a matter of fact, we were operating at a loss. The hotels, in other words, were great fun to own, but I still had to ask myself the hard-headed executive's bottom-line question: What profit a man that maketh no profit?

We finally reached some important decisions. We decided, as I indicated earlier, that we would not buy any more *old* hotels, whose upkeep had become prohibitively expensive and whose profitability in the modern market was constricted at best. We also decided that rather than pull out of the hotel business or merely try to maintain the status quo, we would attempt to become a major factor in the hospitality industry. We had put a hell of a lot of money into our hotels, and, despite our losses, the notion of pulling out at that point ran against the Carlson grain. We decided, instead, to expand. There would be significant economies of scale, for one thing; for another, we felt that a large group of hotels could position and market itself nationally—and, eventually, worldwide—much more effectively than a small one.

We hired Jorgen Viltoft, who was then a senior vice president with the Marriott Corporation in Washington, D.C., to head up our rededicated hotel activity. A native of Denmark, Jorgen was a polished hotelier with a degree in hotel management from the Sorbonne. Interestingly enough, way back in the middle 1950s, he had served as director of food and beverage at the original Radisson in Minneapolis. Now his job was to tighten up the operations of several Radissons, and facilitate our expansion into new territories both in the United States and abroad.

In the hotel business, as in many of our others, we did not, as a company, start out as experts—but we learned plenty through time and experience. We learned, for example, that we could make money restoring (not owning) grand old hotels through CSA, Inc., our design and construction division headed by Ann Richardson. We learned, from our experience in Duluth and elsewhere, the wisdom of bringing in solid, responsible, and prominent local partners. We learned that in our continuing expansion our interests were usually best served by limiting our ownership to ten or fifteen percent—and, in some instances, maintaining no ownership at all, providing instead only management services. We learned, some time later, under our current hospitality division chief, Juergen Bartels, the profit-making power of tightly controlled franchising agreements. (When all of our ancillary companies are available to a franchised Radisson, the improvement in occupancy and public acceptance is remarkable.)

We learned as well that there was value in maintaining and enhancing the local character and individuality of our increasingly far-flung properties. Rather than making sure that each of our hotels looked just like the others, we discovered that it made good marketing sense to emphasize our differences. Hence our eventual slogan: "Radisson Hotels. A Collection. Not a Chain."

I personally insisted—seasoned innkeeper that I'd become—on a few points of perhaps lesser overall importance, but of importance nonetheless. I demanded, for instance, that everyone from a Radisson hotel's senior manager on down to its most recently hired maid greet guests with a cheery hello, that our doormen keep the front curbs clear for arriving guests, that coffee be brewed in the kitchen and brought up fresh to the guests rather than be made from instant powder and hot water in the rooms.

As you might expect, I loved all the hoopla of new hotel groundbreakings and grand openings, with their ceremonial ribbons, colorful balloons, upbeat music, back-slapping local dignitaries, and flashbulb-popping photographers. Such was all part of the "center-of-the-action" mystique promised by Tom Moore. I also loved the exotic adventures that the hotel business and its ongoing expansion occasionally provided me.

I recall the time that Jorgen Viltoft and I flew to the lovely shores of Lake Geneva, in Switzerland, to meet with the legendary Prince Sadruddin Aga Khan. We were interested in building a Radisson hotel on a small but strategically located parcel of land the prince owned along the Nile River in Egypt. The prince had graciously invited us to his palatial Swiss estate to discuss the matter.

Well, as a grocer's boy from south Minneapolis, I assure you that I'd never in my life seen the likes of the prince's estate. The ornate buildings and handsome grounds were absolutely gorgeous. We ate a sumptuous lunch, I remember, in an enormous dining room, with a white-gloved servant positioned behind each guest; each course was served on a solid silver plate. The prince himself was impeccably mannered, gracious, and genial. After lunch we repaired to the manicured gardens to talk business. Our side had suggested that we explore the possibility of a consortium that would build the hotel beside the Nile. As it turned out, however, the prince wasn't interested in any hotel, though, he then told us, he would be happy to sell us the land on which we wanted to build it. The price he suggested for his three-acre parcel was a cool $23 million.

So much for our royal sojourn. The prince's price was firm—and unacceptable. Two-hundred dollars a square foot was appropriate for Nile-side land. Our consortium, however, was planning a more modestly sized hotel; a large, $200-million facility would be required to carry the interest on land that expensive. I told the prince, "Your highness, we are grateful for your hospitality, but I don't think we should waste any more of your valuable time."

And with that, we departed.

O THER EXPANSION ACTIVITY during the late 1960s and early to mid-'70s ranged far and wide in terms of type and size of business, geographical coverage, and both short-term and longer-lasting contribution to Carlson Companies as a whole.

Among the entities we acquired during that period was the May Company, a prominent wholesale grocery house operating here in the Midwest; a growing collection of modest-sized catalog showrooms, including Charles Shaffer, Inc., Naum Bros., and, most successfully, Ardan, Inc., spread all over the country; Superior Fiber Products, Inc., a northern Wisconsin-based manufacturer of hardboard products; the A. Weisman Company, a candy and tobacco-product distributor headquartered in Minneapolis; Milwaukee-based K-Promotions, a producer of specialty advertising products; Jason/Empire Inc., a nationwide merchandiser of telescopes, binoculars, meteorological devices, and sports equipment and apparel; the locally based Maple Plain Company, which provided promotion-fulfillment services for a variety of national advertisers; the self-explanatory WaSko Gold Products Corporation of New York City; and Curtis Homes, a builder of prefabricated residential housing based in Minneapolis.

Some acquisitions were completed after arduous research and lengthy courtships and, occasionally, in the long run, were not worth either the money or the effort. Others were almost breathtaking in both their swiftness and ultimate profitability. In the latter category belonged the Indian Wells Oil Company.

I was not a total stranger to the oil and gas industry. In 1957 I started an annual investing program with Apache Corporation, a highly successful drilling and syndicating company with headquarters in Minneapolis. I was immediately invited to sit on Apache's board of directors, and enjoyed many meetings with chairman Ray Plank and his fine organization.

One day in 1977 I got a call, out of the blue, from a fellow named James E. Ferrell. Ferrell, who owned a propane and natural gas company down in Kearney, Missouri, told me he was looking for a partner in the purchase of a Wichita-based oil company. The company was available at the attractive price of $18 million, but Ferrell said he had been able to raise only $9 million himself. Would I be interested in matching his half of the purchase amount? he wondered.

I am not a man given to impulsive decisions; in areas in which I'm not particularly well-versed—such as oil companies in 1977—I like to move fairly slow and cautiously, armed with all the available facts and options. But this proposal struck me as out of the ordinary, and I had a hunch that I'd better move fast. Right then and there I turned our two-way conversation into a conference call involving Kurt Retzler, who was by that time my top acquisitions adviser, and other senior members of my staff. Ferrell reiterated his pitch for the group, and we invited him up to Minneapolis. A few days later, Ferrell talked to us again, in person. I asked him a few questions face to face, then talked briefly in private to my staff. Fifteen minutes later I told our visitor that we had a deal. The result of that deal was the brand-new Indian Wells Oil Company, in which Ferrell and ourselves were equal partners.

I doubt if we have ever completed a deal so quickly. I know that very few of our investments have turned such a quick, neat profit. Two years later, when we sold Indian Wells to a General Electric subsidiary, we received six times what we had paid for it.

Most of our acquisitions during the '70s, however, were slower to develop and somewhat less lucrative, at least in the short run. We were buying companies at the rate of about four a year. And more and more of the companies we bought were doing business in fields in which we already had an investment—most notably, hospitality, travel, leisure, and food—what I described, collectively, as the "happiness business."

That trend, after a lot of trial and error and several years' worth of refinement, evolved into a policy that eventually served a four-billion-dollar, seventy-five-company conglomerate. That policy presumed a growth-oriented company that was poised for the future on four sturdy legs: the Carlson Hospitality Group (including Radisson and Colony hotels and TGI Friday's and Country Kitchen restaurants), the Carlson Travel Group (including Ask Mr. Foster, P. Lawson, and Cartan Tours), the Carlson Marketing Group (including E.F. MacDonald, etc.), and the Carlson Promotion Group (including K-Promotions, Jason/Empire, and the Gold Bond Stamp Company). It was in those four areas of business that we concentrated our expansion and acquisition activities well into the 1980s. Our objective, simply put, was to be the number-one or -two company in a given industry. (It is a fact of economic life that the leader in any industry enjoys a one- to two-percent bottom-line advantage over the competition.) If we didn't think a company could be dominant in its field, or in some way make a substantial contribution to the synergy of our larger operations, we were not likely to be interested in acquiring it. With that criteria in mind, we also began streamlining our organization through the prudent divestment of companies that no longer fit our overall strategy and structure.

I should add here that I strongly believe that our tremendous growth and development was—and continues to be —facilitated by the fact that we are a closely held private corporation. In some privately held companies, management may have a tendency to fall asleep at the switch, unbothered by the sometimes shrill demands of stockholders, the government, and the press. At Carlson Companies, where (with the exception of the Truman Johnson years) I've held one-hundred percent of the stock, there has never been that problem. The pros of our being private have far outweighed the cons.

We have been able to concentrate, for instance, on building assets, not earnings per share. And since there has been no stockholder pressure for dividends and higher stock prices, all of our earnings could be ploughed back into the company. Our private status has given us, in addition, a tremendous flexibility in our expansion. When an acquisition opportunity has arisen we've been able snap it up with a swiftness a public company couldn't hope to match—and usually without attracting any more attention than we felt would be tactically desirable. We have also benefitted from a board of directors that supplies invaluable expertise, advice, and counsel in several critical areas of management, yet, believing that management knows best about the various particulars of the business, lets management run the show. In my opinion, a board telling management to do its bidding is both absurd and intolerable. Management works day in and day out in the business, while board members come around only once every month or quarter; despite the latter's best intentions, they can't possibly know as much as management knows about the business. If management is crooked or incompetent, the board, of course, has an obligation to make the appropriate changes. But short of that kind of situation, the board must leave management decisions to management. Our board always has, and there's no question in my mind that we've been the better for it.

I have been careful, moreover, to bring together a group of top executives who could advise me in our daily activities, including such important areas of the business as acquisitions. Instead of the Executive Committee, as such groups are called in many corporations, I have called mine the Finance Committee—in part, so not everyone in the company would want to be on it. That group, meeting with me once or twice a week, comprises a small group of my top staff people. Each looks at, say, a possible acquisition from his or her own perspective—from the perspective of tax policy, for example, or the law—and comments accordingly. Sometimes, sure, I'll count the votes on a particular issue and say, "O.K., it was eight in favor and one against, but I'm the one against and I carry nine votes." But that doesn't happen very often. These are smart, insightful people who know their business inside and out, and if I can't persuade them to accept my argument, then I usually figure that I'd better rethink my position.

Even in the area of plotting strategy and tactics, our growth has been remarkable. Decades ago, when we were just starting out, Joe Hunt would argue from an operational standpoint and I would argue from the point of view of sales.

He and I would be the only ones at the table—an undiversified committee of two.

CHAPTER FIFTEEN

The "Impossible" Billion Dollar Goal

IN THE FORTY YEARS between 1938 and 1978, our company grew steadily—some would say spectacularly—at a rate of thirty-three percent compounded annually. In retrospect (though I probably would have made the same assessment at any point during the span of those forty years), I believe that such growth was the result of a combination of several potent factors, including the skill and hard work of a lot of dedicated people, our ability to recognize and exploit a promising opportunity when we saw it, and, not necessarily least among the various factors, the presence of my lucky star.

I credit goal-setting as the single most important contributing factor to our record. Goal-setting includes, of course, a carefully detailed analysis of that goal, how it will be achieved, and the capital required to achieve it. For many years we set goals in five-year increments, with Year One broken down by months, Year Two by quarters, and Year Three semi-annually. For the final two years, only the sales necessary to achieve the five-year revenues and profits were projected.

You could make the case that most if not all of those elements were present in our acquisition, for example, of the TGI Friday's restaurant chain and its subsequent development. Perhaps it was predictable, if not inevitable, that at some point we get into the restaurant business in a major way. I had been familiar with the business end of restaurants since my college days, when I delivered soda pop for my father's distributorship, and, working with thousands of grocers over the years, I had an intimate knowledge of the food industry. More recently, we had acquired the May Company and had thereby become directly involved with the wholesale distribution of food. Finally, we had also, by way of our hotel activity, become actual participants in the restaurant business, at least to the extent that restaurants—such as the Flame Room in the original Minneapolis Radisson and the New York-style Haberdashery cafes in several of our other hotel locations—were part of our budding hospitality division.

One day in 1975, at a time when industry analysts were pointing to fast-food chains as the hottest-growing segment of the restaurant market, I happened to have lunch at a small New York City establishment with sprightly red-and-white awnings above the windows, walls full of oddments and antiques, and a lot of hamburgers on the menu. More interesting to me from a business point of view, the place was packed with a young and generally affluent-looking crowd. The restaurant's catchy, if somewhat unusual, name was TGI Friday's.

While I enjoyed the little restaurant and could appreciate its obvious popularity, I didn't give it any further thought when I returned to Minneapolis. Then, about three days later, I got a call from a fellow at Oppenheimer & Company in New York, who told me that a small chain of popular restaurants was looking for money with which to expand. The name of the chain was none other than TGI Friday's. A short while later, after a look at the restaurant chain's numbers, I told Oppenheimer we were interested in learning more.

Friday's, it turned out, had an interesting history. Its founder was a Manhattan-based salesman named Alan Stillman, who had recognized the demand for a casual, attractive, singles-oriented restaurant and bar in his First Avenue neighborhood. Exploiting that demand, he created his own cafe, filled it with antiques and other interior curiosities, hung distinctive red-and-white awnings over the windows, and gave the place a memorable name. Stillman's "recipe" worked. That original Friday's had been an immediate success.

Well, word of a good, strong, money-making idea has a way of spreading quickly beyond its original neighborhood. So, before long, investors in other parts of the country became interested in Stillman's concept and opened franchises in Memphis and Nashville, Tennessee, and Little Rock, Arkansas. The Memphis franchise (or "store," as individual restaurant units are called in the business) was patronized by a pair of Boise Cascade employees named Dan Scoggin and Walter Henrion. The two men, as it happened, were a couple of would-be entrepreneurs looking to find the right enterprise. In that Memphis Friday's one day, Scoggin said to Henrion, "We've got to do something—even if it's something foolish like this."

Though neither man knew anything about the restaurant business, they contacted Alan Stillman, paid $5,000 down for a franchise in the booming market of Dallas, Texas, and raised about $650,000 to build a new Friday's store from scratch. When construction was completed in 1972, the place was the chain's largest and most elaborate franchise, featuring two-hundred-forty seats on several levels, an elevated bar in the middle, an astonishing array of antiques and artifacts, and a pressed tin ceiling that alone set back the young entrepreneurs about $10,000. That restaurant also boasted what at the time was described as "the world's tallest telephone booth"—a $15,000 double-decker that, despite the phone company's initial misgivings, contained the greatest revenue-producing pay phones in Dallas. The franchise itself was enormously successful from the moment it opened its doors.

Eventually Scoggin and Henrion opened additional Friday's franchises in a half-dozen other markets, including Houston, Texas, and Atlanta, Georgia. Then, in 1975, they felt the squeeze of the recession. Desperately needing capital, they approached Oppenheimer for help; Oppenheimer eventually contacted us.

As I say, I was interested. I dispatched our acquisitions chief Kurt Retzler to Dallas to get a first-hand look at the business and its numbers, and Retz came back with a positive evaluation. Both sides then sat down for what turned out to be literally hundreds of hours of negotiation that seemed to end in a stalemate. Wondering what was causing the delay, I finally stuck my head into the conference room. I asked the Dallas group if giving them control of the Friday's board of directors over the next five years would break the deadlock. When they said it would, I said, "You've got it." Just like that, we had an agreement.

Stillman, the chain's founder, and various other stockholders were bought out for cash. I insisted, however, that Scoggin and Henrion continue to run the operation under terms of a five-year earn-out agreement. They would receive, in addition, a series of bonuses and extra benefits for maintaining an accelerated expansion schedule that we had developed.

The Friday's chain expanded all right. Within three years there were stores in some thirty cities from coast to coast, and all of them were successful. One store, in Fort Lauderdale,

Florida, featured a three-story telephone booth and yearly receipts totaling more than $4 million, thus topping its spectacular Dallas prototype in both categories.

TGI FRIDAY'S developed into what we believe to be the premier restaurant company in the nation. In addition to its own stores, Friday's eventually operated several old-fashioned "soda-fountain" style restaurants called Dalts. Together with our Country Kitchen family restaurants—which we acquired in 1977 and soon accounted for hundreds of locations in the United States and Canada—they represented our considerable investment in the restaurant trade. Their expansion underscored our determination to become a significant player in whatever field of endeavor we entered.

The restaurants became a major part of our Hospitality Group, which grew, of course, out of our Radisson hotels. In the 1980s, the Radisson Hotel Corporation had become a remarkable example of rapid growth and market penetration in its own right. With almost two-hundred properties around the world by the end of the decade, Radisson was, in fact, the fastest-growing hotel company in the country.

The acceleration of Radisson's growth in recent years further illustrates that potent combination of factors I mentioned at the beginning of the chapter. After its initial expansion during the '60s, our hotel division, though continuing to grow, began to fall behind other, faster-growing parts of the corporation; its contribution to the corporate synergism, in other words, had become smaller relative to its Carlson counterparts. We had learned a great deal about the hotel industry during our first several years in the business, but we were no longer expanding as rapidly as I thought we ought to.

About that time we were getting into restaurants in a big

way, as well as adding companies in several other areas of the corporation, and I was becoming more and more concerned about having too many persons reporting to me. Over the course of several decades, I'd determined that the greatest number of people a chief executive should have reporting to him is seven. More than seven, and the CEO will probably have trouble keeping everyone straight and everything on track. So it was that I decided at that point to divide our various divisions into four groups. As part of that reorganization, I placed our hotel and restaurant operations into the Hospitality Group and, some while later, hired a bright young man named Juergen Bartels to run it.

"J.B.," as we like to call Bartels, grew up in the hotel business. He began his career as a sixteen-year-old food-and-beverage apprentice at his uncle's hotel in Bremen, Germany. From there he went on to carve a handsome career for himself in Canada and the United States. In 1979, at the ripe old age of thirty-nine, he became president of the Ramada Hotel organization, which is where he was when we hired him to head our Hospitality Group in 1983. His precocious career experience aside, what impressed me about J.B. was his combination of brains and enthusiasm. Here, I thought, was the fellow we need to make the Hospitality Group grow! It was our good fortune that we found him at that critical stage of our development.

I wasn't misled by my initial impressions. Under Bartels and John Norlander, whom we hired as Radisson Hotel Corporation president in 1975, our position in the hotel market began to rise dramatically—from the rank of fifty-sixth to the rank of fifteenth in a period of only three-and-a-half years, according to authoritative industry sources. Our aim, of course, was (and still is) to be first in the upscale hotel industry.

The second and third legs of what, during the middle '80s, I visualized as a four-legged stool were, meanwhile, giving us that kind of market significance.

The Carlson Travel Group, for its part, had become the largest travel organization in the world, with more than seven-hundred individual agencies serving both the corporate and the individual traveler. Back in the middle '70s, we decided that having learned a good deal about travel operations through our various incentive companies and our own internal incentive programs, we wanted to expand into broader travel applications. We began to look around at some of the larger players in the field.

In 1976, we looked with particular interest at First Travel Corporation, a Van Nuys, California, based organization that was then doing about $50 million worth of business through its Ask Mr. Foster units around the country. First Travel was the baby of still another bright, young entrepreneur, one Peter Ueberroth. When our man Retzler expressed our interest in First Travel to Ueberroth, the latter replied that he just might be willing to sell at an opportune moment.

As events turned out, that moment arrived in 1979, not long after Ueberroth was named organizer-in-chief of the 1984 Olympiad in Los Angeles. His new job would be truly Olympian, and would leave him little time and energy to run a huge travel business. In late 1979, he sold us fifty-five percent of his company, and five months later he sold us the rest. Peter's brother John and several of his top employees joined us as part of the acquisition—and, suddenly, we were a major force in the industry.

The Carlson Marketing Group had grown out of our initial motivation and incentive business. By the end of the 1980s it made us the largest incentive company in the world, with billings of a billion dollars a year. Its scope had become international and included such familiar and respected names as the E.F. MacDonald Company, which we acquired from our old friend Elton MacDonald in 1981. E.F. Mac-Donald Motivation, as we called it, was one of three divisions within the group. The others were the Consumer Promotions Division, which included such early acquisitions as K-Promotions, and the Retail Marketing Division, which included the original Gold Bond Stamp Company.

In 1988, Gold Bond celebrated, appropriately enough, its golden anniversary!

SUCCESS, AS THE MAN SAYS, breeds success, and over time our significance in the few key markets in which we decided to concentrate became an additional powerful factor in our growth.

There was, for one thing, the considerable role that synergism played in the ongoing development of a big and growing company like ours. Synergism occurs when the various individual parts, working together, contribute something to the whole that each part could not accomplish if working by itself. You can imagine, I'm sure, the synergistic possibilities that by the 1980s were inherent in our organization. Our incentive companies, to use an obvious example, developed festive trips for their clients' employees; the trips could be arranged by our travel agencies, and could involve, where appropriate, accommodations provided by our hotels.

Our size, moreover, increased the depth of the many possibilities. If one of our travel clients stipulated a deluxe hotel in a particular city, there would be a pretty good chance that Radisson would have one of its deluxe properties in that location. If the client desired less expensive accommodations, there would probably be a less expensive Radisson Inn in the vicinity.

The personnel implications of our size and success were similarly obvious. During a discussion on the subject of staff, I once asked our Radisson boss John Norlander where he was finding so many highly talented managers. Managing a hotel is one of the more challenging assignments I can think of, and, frankly, until fairly recently, finding good men and women to handle that job was a problem for us. John's answer was instructive. He said, "We're the fastest-growing hotel chain in America right now. Thus every good, aggressive manager in the country would like to join us because they know that as we get bigger, their own careers will grow, too." Good managers make good hotels, which, in turn, make a great—and growing—hotel corporation.

Our situation had become, over the years, like that of a college football powerhouse, whose many and increasing number of victories serve to attract more and more good players who, in turn, help perpetuate the team's winning record. People like playing for a winner. People, for that matter, like their *spouses* playing for a winner. Even aside from a growing salary, bonuses, awards, and other tangible benefits, there is that *in*tangible—but very powerful—factor called prestige.

From a purely personal point of view, I can tell you that nothing satisfies me more than seeing our good men and women developing their careers and thus providing themselves and their families with both the income and the stature that comes with their company's continuing achievement. It lends a stability to the company that helps quiet the owner's nerves.

Our function here, as far as that's concerned, has always been to grow, to develop new opportunities, to earn more money, to plough that money back into the company so that we can continue to grow. We're not surgeons, whose success can be gauged by the number of human bodies we've saved or repaired. Nor are we lawyers, whose value can be determined by the number of cases we've won for our clients. We're business people. We measure our success by how much business we do—or by how much *more* business we did today than yesterday. With its dollars, the public decides who grows and who doesn't. Our bottom line is the means by which we tally up the public's "votes."

Which brings us back, in a somewhat roundabout way, to still another key factor in our growth. That factor has been our use of specific—and often daunting—goals.

In December 1972 I gathered our top executives together at the then-recently completed Radisson Inn Plymouth near our headquarters. I began my talk with a question: "How much is a billion?" Before anyone had time to reply, I said, "I'll tell you what a billion is. A billion is the sales goal of the Carlson Companies by 1977. That is, in the five short years between January 1, 1973, and December 31, 1977, we want to reach a sales level of one-thousand-million dollars per year!"

The context of that announcement had not exactly been conducive to bold new initiatives. The nation was on the downward slide of a recession that many economists were predicting to be the worst since the Great Depression. Furthermore, the investment that would be required to reach such a goal would be enormous, and the risk implied by such an investment would be great, even in the best of times. But if we were to grow—if we were to be as important a force in our diversified state as we'd been as a single-product company—we would have to take that huge risk and make a commensurate commitment.

King-sized goals lend an excitement to top people eager

to meet a challenge. It carries an emotional appeal far greater than that of quitting early to play golf or spending long weekends at the lake. Accordingly, I told the assembled executives:

"Those in this room, plus a few more people that are important to your operations, will have to eat, sleep, and dream your quotas. When you're brushing your teeth, when you're driving to work, when you're listening to the choir in church, your mind will be searching for the ways and means to achieve your goal."

A billion dollars was too large an amount for the little slips of paper I used to write my goals on and tuck into my wallet. But the huge sum's presence on company signs, memos, and banners—and in the hearts and minds of our workforce—had a powerful, almost electrifying effect. Our thousands of executives and employees responded with a tremendous effort. In the first of the five years of the drive, our sales topped the projected $375-million level—though just barely. The following year, the annual corporate quota was more comfortably surpassed, and by the end of 1977 we had shot past the three-quarters-of-a-billion mark.

In December 1978 I was very pleased to announce that we had exceeded our "impossible" billion-dollar goal by more than $40 million. I also announced that all of our top executives, from our many far-flung divisions, along with their spouses, would be rewarded with an all-expense-paid, eighteen-day trip around the world. The following May, we would fly to Rome, then onto India and Thailand, then finally our ultimate destination of Japan. Solid-gold rings with "$1,000,000,000" etched on the sides and holding a sparkling one-carat diamond would be presented to each executive in Tokyo.

By that time, of course, we would already be en route to our *second* billion dollars.

CHAPTER SIXTEEN

A Private Company with Public Concerns

N O MAN IS AN ISLAND, said the poet. No company is an island, either—not even a closely held, independent-minded, multibillion-dollar company like ours. We are an integral part of the communities in which we do business. We draw our workforce from those communities, and sell them our goods and services. We abide by their laws, rely on their services, and pay their taxes. We think that all of us are enriched by the relationship.

Developing a company from scratch, however, is a difficult, virtually all-consuming activity. Like an entrepreneur's family, his community may be at least temporarily overlooked in the process. Except, of course, at tax time, or in the unfortunate event of a fire or break-in at his office or plant, the community in which he operates is something he often takes for granted.

The entrepreneur is, of course, providing valuable contributions to the community as he's building his business. The day-to-day operation of his company translates into jobs for the community's workers and tax revenues for its treasury. Growing companies generally mean growing communities. But the entrepreneur is usually hard put to spare much of his personal time and attention. What's more, he is ploughing every dollar he earns back into the company.

That precious supply of capital is critical to his company's survival. If the company is privately held, he has no access to public funds, and thus every dollar he earns has to be dedicated to the care and feeding of his business.

I know. I've been there. For more than fifty years, most of my energy—not to mention most of my working capital—has been directed toward the business I started from scratch back in 1938. I had my individual causes and charities, but I was very jealous of my time and money.

By the 1960s, however, Carlson Companies had become a prominent member of the Twin Cities' corporate community. Gold Bond stamps were household words. Now, in addition, our newly constructed world headquarters was an eye-catching complex on Highway 55 in suburban Plymouth, and our expanded and improved Radisson hotels were popular local establishments. In Twin Cities business and civic circles alike, we were known as a fast-growing company on the move.

Not surprisingly, I began to be approached for help in funding several major projects here in town. The Twin Cities of Minneapolis and St. Paul were in the process at the time of breathing new life into their downtowns and their various amenities, and the price tag on this rejuvenation was substantial. Several of the projects, such as the new Tyrone Guthrie Theater and Orchestra Hall in Minneapolis, were intended from the start to be nothing less than world-class cultural facilities. I was not, frankly, looking for fresh ways to spend my time and money, but the pressure from my peers, many of whom were close friends of mine, was considerable. Furthermore, I wanted Carlson Companies to be a good corporate citizen—to do its part to keep the community vibrant—so we began contributing our fair share to many of those ambitious projects.

In 1959 I had established the Curtis L. Carlson Foundation to handle the distribution of our charitable contributions. Some years later, I became a charter member of a loosely knit organization known as the Five Percent Club. Promoted locally by the Dayton brothers, of the highly respected Minneapolis-based retailing and philanthropic family, the Club's several corporate members regularly donated five percent of their pre-tax earnings to charity. Five-percent was then the maximum amount the Internal Revenue Service permitted a business to donate to such causes and receive a tax credit.

I liked the five-percent idea for a couple of reasons. It established a reasonable and realistic guideline for a corporation's charitable donations, and it provided a very obvious linkage between a company's growth and its philanthropy. The greater a company's revenues, the larger its charitable contribution—which, to my way of thinking, was not only fair but deeply satisfying. As it's turned out, our own contributions have, indeed, grown along with our profits. By the middle 1980s, for example, Carlson Companies donations, as determined by the five-percent formula, totaled some $6 million.

Cumulatively, over the past quarter-of-a-century, I'm pleased and proud to say our company's five-percent contributions have amounted to more than $40 million.

I HAVE BECOME, over the past several years, one of the biggest local boosters of the Five Percent Club, now known formally as the Minnesota Keystone Awards. At this writing, more than two-hundred Minnesota-based companies are contributing between two and five percent of their annual profits to charitable causes and institutions. Two percent is double the national average. Still, I can't help but think: if our fifty largest home-based corporations *all* gave five percent, what a boon that would be for Minnesota!

I've also become an enthusiastic proselytizer of the five-percent gospel in other communities around the country. In Louisville, Kentucky, and Sioux Falls, South Dakota, for instance, I've helped business leaders establish clubs. I tell my friends out there that a lot of good local causes need their help. I tell them, moreover, that we in business can almost always do a better job in the community than can big government. We're closer to the problems, we're more creative in our solutions, and we're certainly more dollar-wise than most of the federal bureaucrats. I point out that our private philanthropy pays a more favorable rate of return than our public tax dollars—that dollars spent locally do more for the community's well-being than tax dollars sent off to Washington and returned greatly reduced.

Not that a five-percent, or even two-percent, formula is appropriate for everyone. I strongly urge new or struggling companies *not* to try to give five percent of their earnings to charity. Better they wait, I advise them, until they're on solid financial ground—at which time they can be all the more generous to their communities. I don't, as far as that goes, recommend that many companies contribute up to the ten-percent limit now allowed by the IRS. Old-line, cash-rich companies may be able to afford that kind of giving, but it doesn't make sense for the rest of us. For publicly held companies I would say that ten percent is simply out of the question.

Giving money away, even with the help of a formula, can be almost as complicated a task as making it in the first place. Systems and procedures are required. My daughter Marilyn, a very astute business person in her own right, used to handle most of our corporate-giving activities by herself. Now we have a pair of full-time staffers who evaluate the numerous requests. As you might imagine, we receive an enormous number of grant requests every day. All the various requests are reviewed by our staff, which passes along its suggestions to our charitable-giving committee, which meets four times a year and passes along its recommendations to me. The final decision is mine.

When I evaluate a request for assistance, I ask myself, first of all, if the cause is indeed one better handled by a private gift than by public revenues. Second, I try to determine just how effective our gift might be. Will our gift help make the recipient self-sufficient—which, I believe, is the noblest, most beneficial use of philanthropy—or will it merely allow the recipient to hang on until the next donation? Many worthy causes will never be self-sufficient, and we fund some of those along with the others. I am convinced, however, that our money is most effectively spent on those that can.

Over the years our foundation's efforts have been primarily directed toward organizations, institutions, and individual projects within the larger areas of education, community services, and the arts. At the same time, we have given, when we've felt it appropriate, to causes spanning much broader categories of concern. These causes have included such diverse and geographically scattered institutions as the International Diabetes Center in the Twin Cities, the National Conference of Christians and Jews headquartered in New York, Smith College in Massachusetts, the Royal Swedish Academy of Sciences in Stockholm, and the Carlson Clinic in Haifa, Israel.

Here at home, where we maintain our international offices and employ a substantial number of our growing workforce, we have found good reason to support the varied likes of the United Way of Minneapolis, the Boys & Girls Club of

Minneapolis, the Shriners Hospital for Crippled Children, the Minnesota Orchestra, the Guthrie Theater, the Minneapolis Society of Fine Arts, the Ordway Music Theatre, the Walker Art Center, Gustavus Adolphus College (in nearby St. Peter), the Walker Methodist Residence, and Hennepin Avenue United Methodist Church.

Occasionally we have gotten involved in projects that, strictly speaking, stretch the common definition of charity, but are critically important to the life of the community nonetheless. More than a decade ago the Carlson Companies joined a half-dozen or so other local corporations to help raise funds to build the Hubert H. Humphrey Metrodome in downtown Minneapolis. The Metrodome would never be confused with an orphanage, yet, fifteen years ago, it seemed pretty clear that, without a new multipurpose stadium, the Twin Cities would have difficulty holding on to its major league baseball and football franchises. Several of us among the community's business leadership agreed with John Cowles Jr., then the publisher of the *Minneapolis Star and Tribune*, that big league sports contribute mightily to both the economic and social health of the community, and that if a new stadium was necessary to keep the Twins and Vikings in town, then we should help get one built. So help get one built we did.

A couple years later, when Calvin Griffith, the long-time owner of the Twins, began considering a move to greener pastures anyway—well, we had to act again. This time, in a drive spearheaded by the energetic Harvey Mackay, we joined a dozen other local firms that bought up literally hundreds of thousands of tickets to force the club to honor its attendance agreements. Eventually, in 1984, my good friend Carl Pohlad bought the Twins baseball franchise from the Griffith family, infused it with fresh blood on and off the field, and happily watched the "new" Twins defy 150-to-1 odds to win the 1987 World Championship.

I should add here that if you have any doubt about the incredible emotional impact a successful big league franchise can have on its community, you weren't in the Twin Cities during and shortly after that incredible World Series, or for the Twins' second improbable World Championship in 1991. All I can say, apropos of the subject at hand, is that whatever we in local business invested in that baseball club over the past several years was paid back in spades—and to a degree that went well beyond any of our wildest expectations.

SOMETIMES, IN ADDITION to helping improve the quality of life in a community, philanthropy involves, on a very personal level, the paying back of an old debt. Such has been the case in our giving to the University of Minnesota.

I have spoken earlier of my feelings about the U of M. I can honestly say that many of the happiest memories of my life hark back to those golden years on campus. It was there that I met and courted the woman who would become my wife, and it was there that I was taught some of the most important lessons I would bring to my career. My degree in economics unlocked doors for me that might never have been opened without it. To say I owe an enormous debt to that institution may sound trite and sentimental, but I have said it often, and always from the bottom of my heart.

I often think of my debt this way: Between 1933 and 1937 I was given a first-rate university education, culminating in that bachelor's degree in economics. For the education and degree I paid the university a grand total of $45 a year in tuition. Even taking into account the depressed economic times, I find the thought incredible. So much information, so much experience, so much *life*—for such a minuscule amount of money. Surely I owe the university and, behind it, the taxpayers of Minnesota a substantial amount of gratitude.

I hasten to add that when I've looked at the university from my perspective as the owner of a major Minnesota corporation, I've always seen more than merely my dear old alma mater. I've seen one of the world's great centers of higher education, the state of Minnesota's single most important social, cultural, and economic resource, and the community's foremost training ground for professional and managerial leadership. In fact, fully fifty percent of the executives of our top home-grown companies have been educated at the university. The truth is, the philanthropy I've directed toward the U of M has been inspired by healthy amounts of both personal gratefulness and corporate self-interest.

In 1986 I personally gave the University of Minnesota a check for $25 million, which, I was told, is the largest single gift ever given a public university. At the same time I agreed to lead an unprecedented drive to raise, over the course of the following three years, no less than $300 million, by which we hoped to insure the institution's ongoing academic excellence. The fund drive itself was believed to have been the most ambitious such effort ever mounted by a public university. By the middle of 1988, I was delighted to say we had raised more than $305 million!

Among my specific concerns at the university have been its prestigious business school and its institute of public affairs. The reason for my interest in the business school should be obvious. And that interest has not been diminished by the new name so graciously given it by the university in 1986: the Curtis L. Carlson School of Management. As I told the university's regents when the announcement was made, sharing my name with its school of management was an honor I'd treasure above all others. It was my hope, I told them, that the institution bearing my name would be a mecca for would-be entrepreneurs from all over the country. More recently, I was pleased to give $10 million to kick off a fund drive for a brand-new Carlson School facility.

My interest in the school of public affairs goes back to my long-time fascination with politics and world affairs. It has to do, in part, with the not-so-academic reason of having met Arleen in a political science class. It has to do, in part, with fond memories of the convocations featuring speeches by prominent politicians and statesmen that were a popular part of campus life during my undergraduate days. For a number of reasons, then, I am proud to list among my contributions to the university a leadership role in raising $12 million for the Hubert H. Humphrey Institute of Public Affairs.

Hubert Humphrey was, as I've mentioned elsewhere, a close friend of mine, and I was delighted to play a part in the new facility that bears his name. Likewise I was proud to dedicate the Carlson Lecture Series to the late Vice President, when the company launched the program with a $1-million donation. Since its inception in 1976, the program has brought to the Minnesota campus for major public-policy addresses such important world leaders as President Jimmy Carter, Vice President Walter Mondale, U.S. Ambassador to the United Nations Jeane Kirkpatrick, and Jihan Sadat, widow of Egypt's President Anwar Sadat.

CLEARLY, THERE ARE PLENTY of reasons for businessmen and women to invest both their time and their money in the community, whether that "community" is confined to the city limits or extends to the ends of the earth. Many of these reasons are nobly altruistic, many are born of an enlightened self-interest, many are combinations of the two—as well as many additional—motivations. Did I mention that giving is good for the ego? And that it leaves the donor with a nice, warm feeling? Believe me, it is and it does.

Whatever the motivation and whatever the reward, the important point is that the successful business leader can be—*should* be—a significant force in the maintenance and improvement of his community. He and his peers have the leadership skills, the management experience, and the financial resources to make a positive difference in the day-to-day life of his society.

The proof, if it's needed, is all around me. The Twin Cities is a vibrant community today in large part because of its progressive private-sector leadership. The metro area is blessed with a disproportionate number of Fortune 500 companies having headquarters here. Some, like General Mills, Cargill, 3M, Honeywell, and Dayton Hudson, have been valued corporate citizens for at least the better part of a century. Others, like Medtronic, Ceridian, and Cray Research, have provided more recent leadership. In most cases, the companies that have made up the solid core of the area's corporate citizenry have understood and acted aggressively on the principle that the health of a business is only as strong as the health of the community that surrounds it.

They also understand what I believe to be the three basic rules guiding corporate philanthropy:

First, giving away company assets must be defensible in terms of the company's current circumstances. Day in and day out the company's leadership is called upon to evaluate demands and determine priorities. More often than not, leadership must decide not between good and bad or necessary and frivolous, but among a number of possibilities, most of which are worthwhile. All of the possibilities must be weighed against the company's ability to stay in business—to continue to provide jobs, produce a marketable product, and attract and retain investors. In other words, the first concern of business must be business. Failing businesses are no help to anyone. In fact, they're a drag on the community, a detriment to the public good.

Second, business, whenever possible, should be involved in activities that promote the public interest. No economic system on earth gives business greater rights than capitalism—the right to start a company, the right to sell goods and services in an open marketplace, the right to make a profit. But with those rights come a number of responsibilities—the responsibility to treat employees fairly, the responsibility to produce and sell safe and effective products, the responsibility to pay taxes. There is, in my opinion, the additional, if less clearly defined, responsibility to give something back to the community.

Third, business should not just react, but should try to be *pro*active. In the area of education, for example: If our schools aren't producing the kind of employees we need, let's not merely complain, let's do something about the situation. If we can't attract out-of-town executives because of our schools' reputation, let's fix the schools (after which the reputation will take care of itself). If we don't like the political system's method for selecting our university's administrators, let's exert our collective corporate leadership to effect a change. As the old saying holds, "If you want to go to the dance, don't wait to be asked."

The Twin Cities has not, by any means, licked all of its

problems. Its business leaders can rest assured that there will always be important projects and worthy causes to which they can direct their charitable energies and philanthropic resources.

Meanwhile, those who have amassed large personal fortunes must understand that with wealth comes an important obligation. We are well-advised, I believe, to heed the dictum of John Wesley, founder of the Methodist Church, who said: "Earn all you can, save all you can, give all you can."

CHAPTER SEVENTEEN

A Journey, Not a Destination

THE LATE 1970S, you may recall, was not the happiest period in our nation's history. Americans were taken hostage in Iran. The Arabs were cranking up oil prices. And, after several years of rampant inflation, economists were pointing to a major recession on the horizon. Referring to the pessimism that seemed to be abroad on the land, President Jimmy Carter told us we were in the grip of a spiritual malaise.

At Carlson Companies, meanwhile, I was beginning to see some uncharacteristic negativism in our ranks. As we made our plans for the beginning of the new decade, one management team after another was coming in with what they called "realistic" projections based on the much-anticipated economic downturn. Much to my surprise and dismay, some of our managers were ignoring our stated goal of $2 billion in revenues by 1982 and actually projecting a drop-off in sales from the previous year. Even worse, they were obviously conditioning themselves and their subordinates to accept a decline in their business as a given, as almost an act of God, as something in whose face they were powerless.

Not liking what I saw and heard, I stopped the planning process in its tracks. I thought hard about what seemed to be happening to the company's state of mind. The next morning I called our executives together and, with some considerable emotion, gave them the following little speech:

"We simply can't surrender to negative thinking. We can't turn around and blame the Arabs. We can't blame Jimmy Carter, the OPEC countries, or anybody else.

"If our business slows down this year, we can only blame ourselves. If you remember your Shakespeare, you'll recall that Cassius said, 'The fault, dear Brutus, is not in our stars, but in ourselves.' I say that, too, because since our company started back in 1938, I can find absolutely no relationship, no correlation between the ups and downs of the economy and the progress of our company. We were born in the Depression, have gone through three wars, several recessions, and a lot of hostile legislation—always our progress has been due to our own efforts, not what was happening on the outside.

"Perhaps the reason for this is that we are not like General Motors. We do not have more than fifty percent of a single market as they do. If there is a recession and car-buying is down, no matter how hard their management works, they are going to sell fewer cars!

"But we're made up of many relatively small companies. The giant target that's out there is a two-trillion-dollar-plus economy. We only want to do a modest amount more than last year. In dollars that's so infinitesimal, comparatively speaking, that by the determined and dedicated efforts of you, our management group, we can lift our company to new heights, regardless of this recession.

"We have a superior company because we have superior people associated with us. Proof of this is the fact that we can boast a record of thirty-three percent compounded growth for more than forty years. Now, of course, with larger dollar amounts, we are only looking for a more modest fifteen percent annual growth.

"So make your adjustment here and your modification there if needed to reach your individual objective—but reach it you can, if you give it everything you've got! Rest assured that your company is going to be a two-billion-dollar operation by 1982. . . and that's a promise!"

Well, a promise is a promise, and we were a two-billion-dollar company by 1982. We lifted our noses out of the nay-saying news accounts, and continued doing what we've always done best—*sell, sell, and then sell some more.* Salespeople must always be optimists. They must always believe in themselves and in what they're selling, and they must never lose sight of their objective. I've often said that obstacles are those things a person sees when he takes his eyes off the goal.

I've also, on more than one occasion, pointed out to my managers that the moment their operation stops selling, it is no longer a Carlson company.

WHILE WE MADE A BIG TO-DO out of our achieving that first billion-dollar milestone back in 1978, we passed the next several billion-dollar marks with relatively little fanfare, in part because that first billion, like the first anything, is most always a special occasion, and in part because we have reached the point at which such incremental growth is simply expected. Our mature corporate culture is predicated on the belief in our unflagging growth, in good times or bad.

A reporter asked me if I was excited about achieving four-billion dollars in sales. I replied that, frankly, I wasn't. We were merely doing what we had planned to do. "Now, if we'd hit the *five*-billion mark at that point," I added, "*then* I would have been excited. Because then we would have exceeded our own ambitious projections."

I mention this, just as I reiterated that late-'70s speech to my managers, because it illustrates a key point about this company: It is always—and has always been—at a stage of *becoming*, never one of completion. Even our most ambitious goals are merely milestones along a journey, not destinations in themselves. There are always new territories to open, additional accounts to sell. There is the rest of the day and tomorrow.

I have, of course, tried to staff the company with managers who shared that concept of *becoming*, with executives who were relentlessly optimistic about the future. For the most part, I believe, I've succeeded. Our most effective managers have never had much time for the status quo. They have not required a kick in the pants to get started in the morning. They've shared my thrill for the chase, and, like me, they've taken a genuine pleasure in making the company go. They've had the spark that has always powered this company—that spark being a burning desire to achieve, to reach the next goal, to make tomorrow's company bigger and better than today's.

As for the continuing leadership of the company I can only say this: Succession is an enormous concern of everyone who has built a company of his own. A few years ago I attended a seminar at Harvard University composed of the chief executives of a number of large privately held corporations. What we all had in common was a tremendous depth of feeling about the continuation of our respective companies that simply wouldn't have been shared by the CEOs of publicly held corporations. The fact that only six companies out of a hundred survive as long as a century only deepened our concern that we appoint worthy successors.

I happen to be very fortunate (again that lucky star!).

I believe there is a significant management talent in my family. I believe that in my daughter Marilyn—and quite possibly in some of my grandchildren, several of whom are just beginning to embark on their careers—there is the vision, the capability, and the desire to keep the business moving forward. There is also the determination, I believe, to keep Carlson Companies headquartered in Minnesota and an active part of the state's community life. It should go without saying that I'd love to have my kids and grandkids experience the same joy in running a dynamic private company that I've had.

At the same time, there is no binding reason why a private company like ours could not go outside both the business and the family for its top management. Our giant Twin Cities neighbor, Cargill, the largest privately held company in the nation, has gone outside for its top leadership at least three times, and Bechtel Construction, the country's second-largest private firm, has an outsider behind the president's desk right now. So moving from inside or family management to professional outside leadership is certainly a viable option when appropriate and feasible.

My feelings about operating a private company should be, by this time, quite obvious. For me it's been the only way to go. Our private status has allowed me the freedom and flexibility to act fast, when opportunities present themselves, and to direct our major efforts toward significant long-term goals, without worrying about short-term earnings, dividends, and stock prices. (We have not, incidentally, declared a common stock dividend since 1957.) Even long-time private companies occasionally go public, however, and I cannot realistically rule out the possibility for us.

In the short term at least, I see a great deal of leadership talent at Carlson Companies. I also see—both within our ranks and outside of them, in our nation's business schools and in the American marketplace at large—a vibrant entrepreneurial spirit that excites me. Here at home I experience it daily in the fresh ideas and can-do enthusiasm of our young managers. Elsewhere, when I'm speaking to students or small-business organizations, I see it in the faces of my listeners and hear it in their questions. Young people especially are fascinated by what we've accomplished here in the past fifty-plus years, and their fascination is by no means academic. They want to learn how *they* can do it, too.

The intellectual curiosity and technical knowledge of this younger generation is often amazingly precocious, reflecting, among other things, the sophistication of modern business education. Still, what impresses me the most about these up-and-comers is their incredible desire to learn and to do.

Not long ago I had the thrill of observing some of our young salespeople, part of our E.F. MacDonald subsidiary, making a presentation to a big account in Detroit. One by one our people got up there in front of that customer and told him why he needed what they were selling. One by one they got up there and very effectively drove the point home. I loved what I was seeing. It struck me that those young people could have been members of our Flying Squadron making their pitches in Denver or Kansas City or New York back in the 1950s. They could, for that matter, have been Harry Greenough and me putting on our razzle-dazzle dog-and-pony show in front of Safeway's executives forty years ago!

The thrill for me was, of course, the unequivocal proof that the new generation was indeed carrying the torch, that these youngsters had learned the lessons of the past and were applying them with snap and intelligence to make a better tomorrow for both the company and themselves.

I have always believed in delegating authority, but never abdicating it. For a hands-on kind of guy like myself, letting go ("abdicating" is a term I still can't stomach) is awfully difficult. It is also absolutely imperative, when the time is right, that I do. Well, what I saw during that E.F. Mac-Donald sales presentation was a lively—and greatly reassuring—reminder that we had reached the point at which I could begin to let up—and maybe even begin to let go.

TODAY I'M GENUINELY looking forward to the time when I can enjoy a little more freedom from the cares and concerns of running a big business. I must find more time for my fundraising efforts, among other things. There are the many important causes and institutions I talked about in the previous chapter to help fund, as well as such dear-to-my-heart interests as the year-long, nationwide New Sweden celebration that took place in 1988. That gala extravaganza celebrated the 350th anniversary of the first Swedish settlement in the United States, and honored the enormous contribution to American society of countless Swedes from that day to this. I was greatly honored and privileged to serve as New Sweden '88's honorary chairman. All in all, there is never any shortage of worthy endeavors with which to get involved and raise funds. I consider it a positive sign that none of my friends has as yet taken to crossing the street when he sees me coming!

I would not, as some people undoubtedly would, want the opportunity to start all over again. Building this company from the ground up has been grueling work as well as a lot of fun, and now I'm approaching the time when I'm willing to let the younger crowd have a chance to appreciate both.

Sometimes I wonder, for all the success we've had through our remarkable diversification of the past three decades, what the company might have done if we had concentrated solely on sales incentives and promotion. By the late 1950s, you will recall, the traditional trading-stamp market was saturated. There was simply no place to go with those stamps as the industry was using them at the time. Stamps had become the victim of their own incredible success.

But look around. In the 1990s we may not see many trading stamps anymore, yet the trading-stamp *concept* has never been more potent.

Consider, for example, all those frequent-flyer clubs—virtually every airline in the world has one. The same idea can be seen behind the frequent-guest plans our Radisson hotels and numerous other hospitality companies around the globe have offered. Frequent-flyer and frequent-guest plans are simply today's equivalent of the old-fashioned trading stamp! You fly so many times with a particular airline, and you earn a free ride. You stay so many times at a particular hotel, and you earn a free night's lodging or a related award. Meanwhile, department-store customers earn "points" with their purchases. A certain number of points will entitle the customer to special gifts or travel awards. All of these clubs, plans, and point programs are trading stamps in modern dress. All of them are doing precisely the same thing that stamps have done: provide a powerful incentive to keep the customer coming back for more.

As it happens, our Promotion Group has been a very active player in many of the continuity plans. With our modern computers and systems we have run, for example, the frequent-flyer program for several of the world's airlines, as well as the frequent-guest plans of Radisson hotels and several other hotel organizations. For that matter, we still sell our Gold Bond stamps and a number of other related promotion and incentive programs.

I have no regrets about the paths we have taken. We have achieved far more than I ever, as a young man, dreamed possible. I am grateful for the guidance and direction given me by the Lord and my parents, the love and encouragement provided by my wife and daughters, the loyalty and support of my friends, partners, and employees. I owe a great deal to this country, to the capitalistic system, to my wonderful hometown and its great public and private institutions. Without all of that I doubt whether I would have had the ability to envision my goals in the first place, let alone the opportunity to attain them.

The journey continues. There are still a lot of goals out there, and a lot of work to be done if we're going to reach them.

CHAPTER EIGHTEEN

Succession
and Celebration

ON THE EVENING OF JULY 23, 1988, I was pleased to welcome several thousand friends, colleagues, employees, and family members to a gala celebration of Carlson Companies' first fifty years in business. Entitled, appropriately enough, "Celebrate!", the extravaganza filled much of the massive Civic Center in downtown St. Paul, Minnesota, which had been specially converted into a huge formal "dining room," entertainment center, and exhibit area for the occasion. The entire affair was meticulously organized and flawlessly presented by a large group of talented persons headed by my daughter Marilyn Nelson.

It was, I believe, an affair to remember. The dinner, prepared by a collection of top Radisson chefs from around the world, featured smoked salmon with sweet dill mustard, native Minnesota turkey on wild rice pancakes, and "Summer Celebration" raspberries, strawberries, and blueberries with sabayon sauce. A complete orchestra and dazzling ensemble of dancers provided lively entertainment, and several of our executives spoke to the gathering on the future of the business. The legendary Bob Hope, still one of the funniest men on earth, was on hand to remind us not to take ourselves *too* seriously.

Most important as far as I was concerned, the celebration provided me with the opportunity to express my appreciation to the people who have helped make Carlson Companies what it is. Many of those people—employees, suppliers, advisors—I will never know personally. I can only trust that when Hope crooned a special rendition of "Thanks for the Memories," those folks who were present knew that the song was for them as well as for those individuals who were honored by name.

Thirty-one men and women were singled out during the celebration, and they will never be forgotten for their contributions to the success and growth of the company. Twenty-six of them were key players during the Gold Bond years—roughly 1938 through 1966—when the corporation was primarily a stamp company. Collectively, these individuals provided a foundation on which others have built the modern company. Individually, they were being honored as the charter members of the Carlson Hall of Fame.

They were my brothers Dean and Warren, who were instrumental in so many ways, but especially in Gold Bond's efforts to become first a national and then an international operation; my first two executive secretaries, Dee Kemnitz and Ann Richardson, who went on to become top-level advisors and executives in their own right; John Heim, Chet Krause, and Kurt Retzler, providing decades of sound legal, financial, and merger-and-acquisition advice; talented and dedicated operations persons Doris Campbell (my recently retired executive assistant), Jim Carlson, John Ford, Mary Golfus, Joe Hunt (the original "Mr. Inside"), Frank Larsen, Warren Lorenz, and Fay McCall; and some of the greatest salesmen who ever lived—Ed Brennan, Dulyn Butler, Maurice Gold, Harry Greenough (my successor as president of Gold Bond), Orville Hammer (leader of the Flying Squadron), Glen Johnson, Irv Messerschmidt,

Gordon Pearson, Bill Schaffer, Elliot Srebrenick, and Lloyd Thompson Jr.

In addition to the twenty-six Carlson Fellows, we cited five Honorary Carlson Fellows for their important contributions during the early years of our diversification. They were Larry Golden, the crackerjack E.F. MacDonald salesman; Matthew Levitt, whose wise counsel began long before diversification, who's been a member of our board almost since its inception, and who was particularly important when we sailed into uncharted waters; Carl Pohlad, my old friend and banker, who demonstrated confidence in our operations and plans before most people did and who has also been a long-time advisor and board member; Phil Ousley, who played a key administrative role in the critical E.F. MacDonald merger; and Jorgen Viltoft, who, as first president of our Radisson Hotel Corporation, took the initial important steps in transforming a handful of miscellaneous properties into a collection of thirty-two hotels before he retired.

The debt owed all of these persons is incalculable. It was thus my pleasure that gala evening to thank them not only for the memories, which are bright and warm indeed, but for the company's success, which without their energy, dedication, and ability, would never have happened.

I N O N E S E N S E, "Celebrate!" marked the end of an era. We were an organization that, though proud of its past, was charging as fast as it could into the future. Great changes and challenges lay ahead as we embarked on our second fifty years.

As we celebrated in St. Paul that night, work was already under way on our spectacular new World Headquarters in Minnetonka, Minnesota, on the far west side of the Twin

Cities. Indeed, only ten months later, during three days in June 1989, more than three-thousand guests helped inaugurate the facility during its official grand opening—still another festive occasion for Carlson Companies. (We had broken ground for the complex on July 11, 1987.)

Located near the busy intersection of interstate highways 394 and 494, only fifteen minutes from downtown Minneapolis, the new World Headquarters would be the anchor of an eventual $650-million, three-hundred-plus-acre development comprising more than 3.5-million square feet of office, hotel, retail, and residential space, all of which is expected to be completed by the end of the decade.

The structure was erected on the western tip of about a thousand acres of land I began buying in individual parcels in the Minneapolis suburbs of Minnetonka and Plymouth many years earlier. It was farmland back then, in the late 1940s and early '50s, and neither suburb was much beyond a semi-rural bedroom community. Highway 12 (now Interstate 394) was a major east-west thoroughfare, but west of Highway 100, which skirted the inner ring of Minneapolis's western suburbs, there was little in the way of commercial development. Nonetheless, I had a premonition. In my mind's eye I could see the area someday flourishing as an industrial and commercial center. I also had a vision of our company occupying a particular three-hundred-acre triangle along Highway 12 (at what is now the intersection of I-394 and I-494). We did build a headquarters facility on the northeastern end of the thousand acres in 1962. About the same time I sold some of the acreage to the state highway department for the eventual development of I-494. The new interstate helped lead in turn to the development of the Plymouth-Minnetonka corridor that I'd envisioned.

Our new facility, developed by the Trammell Crow Company of Bloomington, Minnesota, was designed by BWBR Architects of St. Paul, the Urban Design Group of Denver, and CSA, Inc., of Minneapolis. Honestly, it's more beautiful than I ever imagined. Unfortunately, I can't take any of the credit. As a matter of fact, I turned down the first two sets of plans for the complex. After rejecting the second set I told the planners to go ahead and do what they thought was best—and look what they gave me! To say the least, it's a spectacular symbol of what this company has accomplished during the past half-century.

The headquarters complex comprises twin fifteen-story towers with a total of five-hundred-sixty-thousand square feet of office space, a three-thousand-seat outdoor amphitheater, a twenty-two-acre lake, and a lush wooded walking area graced with statuary and wild game. The buildings' exterior surfaces combine champagne-colored reflective glass, a reddish brown polished and flame-cut granite base, a more lightly polished and flame-cut granite tower, and a sloped dove-gray metal roof with twin twelve-foot spires.

Visitors and employees alike seem particularly inspired by the magnificent bronze statue at the head of the landscaped pedestrian mall in front of the complex. The statue, called *Man and His Genius*, was created by the great Swedish sculptor Carl Milles (1875-1955) and purchased from his estate in Stockholm. Measuring about thirteen by thirteen feet and standing atop a fifteen-foot pedestal, the sculpture depicts the mythological winged horse Pegasus and his rider Bellerophen soaring toward an unseen destination. Viewed from the ground, horse and man seem literally airborne, suspended in space, dramatically symbolizing the heroic act of striving toward a distant goal.

When I look at the sculpture, I see the human trying to climb even higher than his winged steed will take him. I see his flight as not only a quest for a perhaps unreachable goal, but a profound longing for personal freedom and individual perfection. That longing, to my mind, lies at the very heart of the free enterprise system and the entrepreneurial spirit, which has driven the growth of our company from its very beginning.

I first saw *Man and His Genius* about twenty years ago. Arleen and I had made a tradition of taking our grandchildren to Sweden when they reached the age of twelve, and our trips always included a visit to Millesgarden, the late sculptor's estate, in Stockholm. Long ago I'd been taken by Milles' work and dreamed of the day when I might install one of his inspiring sculptures on the grounds of our corporate headquarters. *Man and His Genius*, which I saw for the first time about 1970, seemed to symbolize precisely what our company was all about. Finally, in 1989, with our new World Headquarters providing the perfect setting, I commissioned Milles' estate to make a final mold of the work, the last of three in the world.

On June 19, 1990, with the help of Swedish ambassador to the United States Anders Thunborg, then Minnesota Governor Rudy Perpich, a thousand guests and employees, and a clutch of Swedish fiddlers, we formally dedicated the sculpture on its pedestal in front of our new buildings. Among my remarks on *that* festive occasion, I told the gathering that the work speaks eloquently of our company's unending commitment "to reach beyond and outperform yesterday."

Like all great works of art, *Man and His Genius* speaks to each individual in his or her own way, but whatever its personal message, our people say they love the amazing statue. It gives the company a unique personality, they tell me.

Recalling the time so many years ago when the Gold

Bond Stamp Company was personified by the plucky little Scotsman Sandy Saver, I couldn't be happier with the way that personality has evolved.

THE CELEBRATION, construction, and dedication ceremonies during the past few years, however grand and inspirational, were only the most visible manifestation of the end of one era and the beginning of the next for Carlson Companies. On September 29, 1989, I turned the title of president and chief executive officer over to my son-in-law, Edwin ("Skip") Gage. So doing, I formally removed myself from the company's day-to-day operations and became chairman of the board.

The official announcement came as no surprise to anyone either inside or outside our corporate walls. Skip, my daughter Barbara's husband, had been an important member of the Carlson team for more than twenty years, having joined Gold Bond as its first director of marketing development and research in 1968. He had been at my side during our growth and development of the 1980s, first as executive vice president and then as president and chief operating officer. As I told the press in our formal announcement, he had earned his spurs and was well-equipped to lead the company into the twenty-first century. He enjoyed not only my confidence, but the confidence of our top-level managers.

The Carlson Companies, for its part, was no longer a small, one-man operation. The company at that time—the fall of 1989—was generating more than $5 billion in systemwide revenues and providing employment for upwards of sixty-one-thousand people around the world. I was seventy-five years old. Though I was hardly at a loss for either drive or inspiration, it was time for a younger man—Skip was forty-eight when he became CEO—to take over on a daily basis. In any case, my handing over of the chief executiveship was not the same as retiring. As I told employees at the time, I was stepping up, stepping back, but by no means stepping out. The company's leadership transition was, in fact, part of a major restructuring of the family business organization.

My primary objective was to provide for the best long-term interests of both the company and the Carlson family. Toward that end we established, at the time of the transition, Carlson Holdings, Inc. (CHI), which comprises Carlson Companies and the family's real estate operations and investment group. Among other things, the creation of CHI separated the governance of Carlson Companies from its management. The individuals in charge of each of the three CHI holdings (including Carlson Companies) would report to the CHI board, consisting of Arleen, my daughters Marilyn and Barbara, my sons-in-law Skip and Dr. Glen Nelson (who's vice chairman of Medtronic, Inc.), and myself (board chairman). Rod Wilson and Matt Levitt were appointed to the board as advisory directors.

CHI would not administrate; it would only govern. I was adamant on the point. As a matter of fact, its guiding principle was—and still is—summed up by the acronym *NIFO*, meaning "nose in, fingers out." We at CHI would want to *know* everything, but we wouldn't want to *do* anything except make policy as long as sales and profits continued to increase. The day-in, day-out *doing* would be the challenge and responsibility of Skip and the managers of the three operating holdings.

As it happened, however, there was soon another personal concern to deal with. I was not feeling well. My energy was beginning to flag, and I often found myself distressingly short of breath. My doctor told me that one of my coronary arteries was ninety-percent blocked. Given the option of bypass surgery or angioplasty, I chose the latter, which was performed in August 1989. When, a few months later, the artery became blocked again, the only practical choice was quadruple bypass surgery. Dr. Horvald Helseth, a skilled and good-humored Norwegian, expertly performed the difficult procedure at Methodist Hospital in suburban Minneapolis in January 1991.

Thankfully, the operation was a success. I slowly but steadily regained my strength, and within about six weeks of the procedure I was able to return to work on a limited basis. Dr. Helseth warned me that while I'd be feeling pretty good in six months, I wouldn't be back to full strength for about a year. As usual, the doctor was right.

The business, meanwhile, had begun to soften in spots, to lose some of its momentum. Though sales were staying pretty much on track, our profits dropped dramatically in 1990 and again in '91. The crisis in the Persian Gulf had combined with the worldwide recession to put substantial downward pressure on many of our businesses. There were internal problems as well. I noticed, for instance, a disturbing tendency for the sales arm of the business to react to directions from the support staff, when it should be the sales force driving the business. Some of our senior managers, moreover, seemed too willing to use the outside pressures as an excuse for indecision and inaction. I decided that there was no substitute for experience at the helm and began to be active again in day-to-day operations.

Skip was still our CEO, but my daily presence was causing considerable strain. As he expressed it later, Carlson Companies was being run, in effect, by two CEOs at the same time. My daughter Marilyn, in the meantime, was eager to play a more meaningful role in the business. From my point of view, the business had in fact grown too big for a single CEO. What we needed, it seemed to me, was a management team. Trying to find the best path through a very delicate situation, I proposed the creation of an Office of the Chairman in which Skip and Marilyn would serve co-equally as vice-chairs. At that point, Skip announced that he wanted to go into business for himself—to become an entrepreneur in his own right.

I was surprised and disappointed by Skip's decision. At the same time, I could understand, appreciate, and even applaud the desire to be his own boss. That was, after all, the impulse that had driven me for more than fifty years.

Skip wanted to purchase the entire Carlson Marketing Group, but eventually decided to buy three of our marketing companies, all of which were profitable but not essential to the operation of our core businesses. Earlier, in his capacity as chief operating officer, Skip had worked closely with the three companies, so he knew them well. I felt the decision to take on so much responsibility at one time was somewhat risky, but it represented a compromise between Skip's original desire to purchase the whole Marketing Group and what I believed to be a more prudent approach to conserving his capital. On November 8, 1991, we formally announced that Skip was forming his own company, the Gage Marketing Group.

I was now faced with two major worries. The first revolved around my concern for Skip and Barbara and that part of the family. If Skip successfully managed Gage Marketing Group and the new company prospered, I felt the entire family would come together both physically and spiritually. And in fact, my worry aside, I was confident that once Skip got his organization trained and out making sales, Gage Marketing would become an important player in the industries in which he chose to operate.

The second—and more pressing—concern involved Marilyn's ability to learn what I believed she had to know in the short time we had left. Bright, well-educated, and highly motivated, Marilyn would be the ideal candidate to eventually run Carlson Companies. Marilyn has always been a super-achiever. She graduated with honors from Smith College in Massachusetts and then studied economics and political science at the Sorbonne in Paris and L'Institut des Hautes Etudes des Sciences Economiques et Politiques in Geneva, Switzerland. She has worked in the securities and banking businesses, sat on the boards of several major corporations (including Exxon and US West), led numerous civic organizations and charity drives, and headed Minnesota's successful Super Bowl Task Force—all this and more in addition to raising a family of her own.

But every expert on the subject of family-business succession has advised that a candidate for the chief executiveship have at least three years of successful outside business experience before joining the family enterprise. Then, according to the experts, the candidate should have not less than fifteen years' experience inside the company, to learn the business from bottom to top. If such an "apprenticeship" was recommended for an average-sized company doing, say, a hundred-million dollars in sales, how much more would there be to learn for someone aspiring to head a multibillion-dollar multinational collection of seventy-five separate companies? Although Marilyn had truly "grown up" with the Carlsons' family business, her corporate managerial experience was clearly not as extensive as the family-business consultants recommended.

I was now seventy-nine years old, with the reduced stamina typical of my age and a breathing problem resulting from my heart surgery. Marilyn was fifty-three. Clearly, neither one of us had the luxury of a fifteen-year training period. Fortunately, Marilyn is a quick learner who I knew would dedicate herself to making every hour pay off. And, indeed, her twelve-hour days and her obvious desire to become an outstanding chief executive representing the second and third generations of the Carlson family finally helped overcome my fears, and she became heir-apparent. She would succeed me as president and chief executive officer.

Of course, we both know that making a success of the upcoming transition will be no mean feat. But Marilyn is entitled, for the sacrifices she'll be called on to make, to the entire family's empathy, understanding, and good will. Anything less would be unworthy.

THE DECISION to establish Carlson Holdings culminated a long period of arduous soul-searching and thought. As I've said many times, what purpose would be served by building the family business if the family itself is eventually divided by it?

There were several possible choices. I considered the option, for example, of breaking up the company and equitably parceling its pieces or the cash among the family members. Certainly this would pass the so-called "fairness test." But Carlson Companies, I decided, was greater than the sum of its parts. Broken up, it would lose both the strength given it by its size and the considerable synergism of its many parts working together. I determined, rather quickly in this case, that it was preferable to keep the corporation in one large, synergistic whole and trust the common sense of my descendants to see and understand the benefits of close cooperation in guarding the assets of their children, their grandchildren, and so on for seven generations, at which point they will, by federal rules, be liable for its estate taxes.

Borrowing an excellent idea from our neighbors at Cargill, I established a proviso stipulating that if the two sides of the family can't agree on a major point of business, the issue will go to formal arbitration. Each side, according to the provision, will appoint an arbitrator, and those two must agree upon a third arbitrator. If the two arbitrators are unable to agree, the third arbitrator will be appointed by the original two arbitrators from a list provided by the American Arbitration Association. I was encouraged by the fact that the Cargill holdings were down to the fifth generation of the family without a single case having been arbitrated. Arbitration as a last resort apparently made everybody more amenable to working out disagreements on a friendly, informal basis.

Looking ahead, I believe that the second generation is going to do just fine via Carlson Companies and Carlson Holdings. If I have lingering concerns, they regard the third generation, whose commitment to the business will likely (and understandably) be diluted by marriage and divergent personal and professional interests. I have seven grandchildren, some of whom I hope will want to join us and help carry on the family tradition. Some family members might at some point want to take the company public but keep controlling interest, which might be to everybody's advantage, so long as the short-term mentality and other equity-market-related pitfalls can be avoided. In any case, such a decision will be up to them.

One thing is certain: I am not going to run the business from my grave. I wouldn't want to if I could. My overriding objective has been to leave my successors and survivors a well-managed, prosperous, growing organization—plus the ways and means by which to equitably share its bounty.

I'm confident we've taken the steps, both as a corporation and a family, to pass on to the next generation a vibrant company based on a solid foundation of top-quality customer service. And that confidence gives me good reason to celebrate the successful passing of the responsibility to my successor and so on for the next five generations.

CHAPTER NINETEEN

Fast-Forward

ONE OF MY long-standing enthusiasms is pictures. Still pictures. Moving pictures. Pictures on slides, on movie film, on videotape. In 1938, the year I started the Gold Bond Stamp Company, I began filming my family with an eight-millimeter camera I'd given Arleen. With a variety of media and upgraded equipment, I've been taking family pictures ever since. Today I have a room filled with slides, film, and tape, and one of the leisure activities I cherish most is organizing and editing all those images into a large but coherent whole. When I'm finished, it will be the story of our family life in pictures, beginning with our marriage and continuing through the birth of our children and many of our grandchildren, to the recent birth of three great grandchildren.

As I direct my attention to the past, however, I can't help but let my mind run fast-forward for a while, exploring the challenges and opportunities that await my successors. I truly believe that they face an exciting and hugely rewarding future. I base that belief on both the state of the company as I write this and the potential for even greater success I see on the global horizon.

At the end of 1993, Carlson Companies could boast systemwide revenues of more than $10 billion, a synergistic network of seventy-five separate corporations, and more than a hundred-thousand employees systemwide. Our Travel and Hospitality Groups were among the top players internationally and growing stronger by the day. The Marketing Group was in the process of re-engineering itself and making satisfactory progress. With a wide variety of high-quality products and services, we were touching the lives of literally millions of consumers the world over every day. According to *Fortune* and other magazines, we were one of the largest privately held corporations in the United States. We were, in short, a robust, steadily growing enterprise strategically positioned for the decades ahead.

Moving ahead in the '90s, the Carlson Marketing Group is a global marketing promotion organization that develops consumer, trade, and employee loyalty-point programs for its clients. Those services range from market analysis and strategic planning to program implementation and evaluation, and amounted to revenues of more than half-a-billion dollars at the end of 1993. It's thrilling and gratifying for me to think that the group's extensive operations grew out of the original Gold Bond stamp concept. Talk about a mighty oak from a tiny acorn!

Our Carlson Travel Group comprises retail, commercial, and incentive travel operations, which brought in more than $7 billion in systemwide revenues in 1993. Its Carlson Travel Network is the largest travel management/agency organization in North America and one of the largest in the world, with more than two-thousand company-owned and franchise locations in the United States, Canada, Europe, and the Pacific Rim. (We changed the name from Ask Mr. Foster to Carlson Travel Network in 1990. We felt the new name better reflects the substance and scope of our entire company and any new enterprises we may add.)

The Carlson Hospitality Group, meanwhile, continues to grow by leaps and bounds as a global force in the hotel, resort, and restaurant business. Today we're better known on the street as Radisson Hotels International, Colony Hotels & Resorts, Country Lodging by Carlson and Country Kitchen restaurants (operated by our Country Hospitality Corporation), and TGI Friday's restaurants. The group's systemwide revenues totaled more than $3 billion in 1993. Individual TGI Friday's store units averaged sales of $3.45 million in '93, the highest sales per unit of any national restaurant chain.

I believe, looking forward, that as significant a role as each group currently plays in its respective industry, each has tremendous opportunity to expand. I've said many times that America by itself is an enormous market, so large and so dynamic that we'll never be able to outgrow it. Even in the heyday of Gold Bond and Top Value, we never even called on one-hundred percent of the mighty U.S. market. Combine that with Canada, Western Europe, Japan, Australia, China, and other existing markets, add developing markets in Latin America, Eastern Europe, the Middle East, and the Pacific Rim—and you have, quite literally, a wide, wide world of potential customers.

I recall again my father's words of years ago. My father was an immigrant from Sweden, a small country of only eight-million inhabitants. In America, working as a wholesale grocery salesman, his territory was the city of Minneapolis, with a population of three-hundred-seventy-five-thousand. He was so proud of my stamp business in the early days of Gold Bond and my ability at that time to sell the program in the five-state area. One night not long before he died, he was in a reflective mood. He said, "All of America will be your territory, whatever you want to sell."

For *my* heirs and successors, I could update those words by saying, "All the *world* will be your territory, whatever you want to sell."

WE SEE OPPORTUNITY for our various businesses in two broad global contexts: among customers who themselves do business on an international basis
and among individual consumers in the various countries.
Our own operations are already extensively global. Overall, Carlson people hail from nearly forty countries and
speak almost thirty different languages. By the end of 1994,
more than a fourth of our systemwide revenues will come
from operations outside the United States.

Our Hospitality Group, to use one very visible example,
is operating in more than twenty-five countries through
management agreements and franchises. Radisson Hotels
International are prestigious "homes away from home" in
dozens of the major cities and resort areas of the world. The
fastest-growing upscale hotel group on earth, the Carlson
Hospitality Group is opening a hotel somewhere in the
world every ten days and will continue to do so for the next
several years. TGI Friday's is on its way to becoming one of
the most successful specialty dining companies in the world.
New franchises have recently been opened in Korea and
Taiwan. In the next decade, additional franchises will open
in Australia, New Zealand, Indonesia, Malaysia, Singapore,
and Japan.

Historically, most TGI Friday's have been company-
owned. Increasingly, however, we've been developing franchise agreements both in the United States and abroad. In
England, for example, where we work with Whitbread and
Company, the giant London-based restaurant, pub, and
brewing corporation, Friday's cafes are already fixtures on
the local dining scene. As a matter of fact, our Covent Gar-
den unit in London has recorded the highest annual sales
total among the system's more than two-hundred locations.

Earlier in this decade Radisson made headlines with

two important international "firsts."

One was our dramatic entry into the international cruise market with the launch of the SSC Radisson Diamond, the world's first luxury passenger ship to incorporate new "semi-submersible craft" (SSC) technology. Resembling an enormous, futuristic catamaran, the Radisson Diamond rides above the water on struts connected to a pair of submerged hulls, its revolutionary design providing both unsurpassed stability and comfort as well as wider decks for expanded accommodations and amenities. Built in Finland at a cost of $125 million in a joint venture with Diamond Cruise Limited, the incredible twin-hulled craft was christened in London in May 1992 and embarked on its maiden voyage to the Mediterranean Sea.

The other notable breakthrough was the opening of the Radisson Slavjanskaya Hotel in Moscow. Not only is the four-hundred-thirty-room facility our initial foray into the fast-changing former Soviet market, it's the first American-managed hotel offering Western-style amenities and advanced technology hitherto unavailable to business travelers in Russia. The hotel—which opened in late 1991 —is the culmination of an extraordinary joint venture between Radisson and Mosintours, the latter a fifty-fifty venture of the City of Moscow and Carlson Hospitality. Its amenities include four American-managed restaurants, state-of-the-art meeting and communication capabilities, an upscale retail shopping complex, and a fully equipped health club with large indoor pool.

For me, the Radisson Slavjanskaya aptly symbolizes the dramatic—and previously unimagined—opportunities that are possible for an aggressive business determined to expand its boundaries. I had traveled inside the former Soviet Union twice prior to doing business there, both times as a tourist, and I must say I never dreamed we'd be doing business in that nation during my lifetime. I remember on one occasion waiting with my wife for an elevator to take us down to dinner from the fifth floor of a major Moscow hotel. We rang and rang the bell, well aware that on the ground floor the elevator operator was sitting idle in his chair, doing his best to ignore us. When we finally reached the main floor via the stairs, we discovered that the implacable operator would only take guests *up* to their rooms, not down from them. "Hotel policy," we were brusquely told.

Until the so-called "Gorbachev revolution," customer service had been simply nonexistent in the Soviet Union (as well as in most other countries of the erstwhile Communist bloc). When Mikhail Gorbachev and his fellow reformers initiated *perestroika*, they opened an enormous new and dynamic market to service companies like ours. There are risks for our companies, to be sure. The situation in Russia is unsteady at best as its people grapple with massive economic, political, and social change. But that's what entrepreneurs do—take risks for rewards. We believe that our risks, however, are manageable, that we are not sailing so far from shore that we can't row back if we have to. Our capital investment in the Radisson Slavjanskaya, for instance, can best be described as prudent. We don't own the hotel, we're simply managing it. If worst comes to worst, we're confident that on a purely business level our involvement in a developing Russian market will only be postponed, not canceled. In the long term, we see many, many possibilities, not only in hotels and restaurants, but, synergistically, in travel and promotion as well. Our people are over there now, working hard to make certain we're in a position to make the most of the possibilities. So far, the response of both the Russian government and the Russian people (eagerly responsive to the opening of good jobs offered by the hotel) has been positive indeed.

I was personally honored to have the opportunity to welcome then President Gorbachev at our Radisson Plaza Hotel in downtown Minneapolis during the Soviet leader's historic visit to the United States in June 1990. Gorbachev was in Minneapolis to speak to the chief executive officers of a number of U.S. businesses that were exploring the possibilities of getting involved in the Soviet economy. We were selected to be his hosts for the meeting because of the ties we'd established with Soviet government agencies and officials as we put the Radisson Slavjanskaya deal together.

That day I couldn't help but think of the hundreds of dignitaries and celebrities who had visited the downtown Minneapolis Radisson since the inauguration of the original structure by President Taft in 1909. Few of those personages, surely, carried as much power, history, and potential for change as Gorbachev.

During our meeting that afternoon I found the Soviet leader to be a very down-to-earth, even humble man who readily admitted the awesome problems facing his country and who was forthrightly seeking outside help. He was not, though, there to beg for our assistance. As a matter of fact, he very emphatically told the American business people that Russians had long memories and that they would remember those foreigners who pitched in during difficult times. As for those foreigners who waited until involvement in the Soviet economy was risk-free and easy, he added pointedly, "We'll remember *you*, too."

Afterward, more than one commentator pointed out the stunning improbability of the leader of the Communist world paying a visit to an arch-capitalist like me, talking business and in a spirit of friendship and goodwill mutually exploring the opportunities of free enterprise. All I can say is, the commentators were right to be astonished. Who could, only a few years earlier, have imagined such an event taking place?

Since Gorbachev's visit, however, another prominent Russian official, Yuri Luzhkov, mayor of Moscow and a close associate of current President Boris Yeltsin, has twice made trips to the United States, on both occasions taking the time to promote Russian-American relations. Luzhkov and I have in fact formed quite a friendship over the past few years, having visited with each other both in Moscow and Minneapolis. In September 1992 I had the privilege of introducing the mayor when he spoke to the Minnesota Meeting in Minneapolis. In September 1993 he was back in town to address the Minnesota International Center at the Radisson Plaza.

On those and other occasions, the two of us have warmly discussed many things, from the business of running hotels and restaurants to the joys of watching grandchildren grow. A chemical engineer and former industrial manager, he clearly understands the needs of business and forcefully articulates the great opportunity offered by what he describes as Russia's "bottomless market." I consider our ongoing relationship, besides the personal pleasure it gives me, another sign that the world is constantly changing— and in some ways for the better.

As for our own recent progress in Russia, I'm happy to report that at the end of 1993 the Radisson Slavjanskaya was running profitably in Moscow, and we had, in addition, begun managing a new Radisson hotel in the beautiful Black Sea resort of Sochi.

THE OPENING of Eastern Europe is one of only several developments and phenomena to make me optimistic about our future. I was pleased, for instance, that we reached—indeed, exceeded—our 1992 goal of $9.2 billion in systemwide revenues a year early. Corrections have been made in individual businesses affected by the Persian Gulf war of 1991 and the global recession, and I firmly believe that we are becoming one of the dominant corporations in our various industries worldwide.

I believe that one of our greatest challenges will be staying at the top of the competitive heap. There is a marked difference in the respective mentalities of companies that are on top and those that are still striving to get there. The top guy understandably wants to maintain the status quo. It's the smaller guy in the fifth or sixth position who's desperate to find a way to do things differently, to change the order of the world. In other words, the top guy is going to be constantly under siege by the smaller guy, and if the top guy is going to remain dominant, he is going to have to be *at least* as innovative as the others. He has to be. He can't afford to be content to repeat what's already being done—even if it was his idea in the first place. He simply has to find a way to do what he does better than it's being done right now. It is this entrepreneurial imperative that keeps a company king of the hill.

Carlson Companies, like all large organizations, is faced with the problems of bureaucracy and inefficiency. However, as big as we are—as big as we *become*—we must never forget that the ultimate success of this business turns on the individual salesperson getting the order and satisfying the customer. We can't count on the old "tried-and-true" products, services, and techniques to make that sale and satisfy that customer. We must always find new and improved wares to sell and new and improved ways to sell and service them. We must always be able to innovate if we want to stay on top.

Though the recession of 1991-'92 caused many of our individual businesses some problems, it should have been no more detrimental to us than the recessions of the past. Carlson Companies was founded during the Great Depression, after all, and we have always found a way not merely to ride out the down-times, but to turn them into an advantage. As a private company, we don't have to worry about shareholders looking over our shoulders, demanding quick fixes at the expense of long-term growth and stability. We can change gears and directions in a hurry. We can bring plenty of persuasive arguments for using our products and services to draw business in the customer's door. We're in the business, we must never forget, of *developing and selling solutions.* When the going is good, we can help our customers do even better. When the going is not so good, we can help them improve their situation. Either way, we have a golden opportunity to make the sale. For a company such as ours there are unlimited opportunities even—or, maybe, *especially*—in a recession. Carlson Companies can, in fact, help other U.S. companies work themselves out of recessionary doldrums.

Each of our three current operating groups and every division within those groups is now required to produce a mission statement. But our mission statements may not fit the conventional idea of a mission statement. We tell our executives to let their minds run wild, to include in their statements everything they could possibly accomplish with their businesses—cost and time be damned. Then we tell them to narrow the scope a little, to explain what of all that "pie in the sky" is possible during the following year and the three years ahead. We used to operate with five-year plans, but have recently switched to three-year "triads"—a more realistic period, given our fast-changing markets. Our executives are not allowed to say, "It can't be done." They must tell us how it *can*. Finally, they must develop a strategic plan containing the specific means by which their stated missions will be accomplished. Clearly, to reach their goals, the divisions and groups must innovate, innovate, *innovate*. In the ferociously competitive global marketplace of tomorrow, creativity and innovation will be more essential than ever to making the sale.

My personal agenda during the exciting times ahead will soon be focused less on the company, as I become satisfied that the people, policies, and procedures now in place will generate the kind of innovative performance necessary to keep Carlson Companies on top well into the next century.

I'm eager, as I said before, to see more of the wide world that holds so many opportunities for the business. Arleen and I have always traveled a lot, but without the constant pressures of the business we'll be able, as our health permits, to spend more time seeing the sights and smelling the flowers along the route. There are, too, all those family pictures to organize and edit.

Then there is the Carlson School of Management at the University of Minnesota, which I hope to help make the leading mecca for fledgling entrepreneurs between Harvard on the East Coast and Stanford on the West. I do not intend to be a full-time teacher at the school, but I'll do whatever I can to help develop and encourage the entrepreneurship curriculum. Do I think we can create entrepreneurs out of whole cloth? Of course not. But I do believe we can provide essential guidance and encouragement for those young people who have the dream, desire, daring, and drive to start their own companies.

I'm sometimes asked if I think entrepreneurs are born or made. I don't believe it's a question of genes either versus or plus the environment, but rather a matter of genes *times* the environment. By that I mean an individual may be born with the potential to be the greatest pianist the world has ever heard, but if that person never gets the chance to sit down at a piano and discover and develop his God-given talent, those prodigious genes will amount to naught. Like that unfulfilled pianist, entrepreneurs must have—or be able to make for themselves—the opportunity to develop and thrive.

Business is still a joy when you see the kind of positive results we're enjoying again at Carlson Companies, but I'm reaching the point where I'd like to watch someone else have the fun. I'll keep my office here on the fifteenth floor of our beautiful headquarters, with its panoramic view of the Twin Cities' western suburbs and, farther in the distance, the downtown skyline of Minneapolis. (I have an office at home, too, but when I ring, no one comes.) I'll be very happy to come into headquarters every now and again, have lunch with my pals, then go over to the university and work with all those bright young people.

But all that is for tomorrow. Today I must attend to business. My daughter, Marilyn Nelson, is at my side now, helping me run the company as vice chairperson of the board. (She has an office just a few feet from mine.) Marilyn will play an important leadership role as we prepare to bring Carlson Companies into the new century. In fact, I believe she will take this company to unprecedented heights, providing the leadership and continuity that I desire. The company will be in good hands and will prosper with Marilyn and our fifty top executives who are all on a long-term incentive program. It is my hope that together they will ensure the continuation of the Carlson culture while meeting the challenges of change, which seems to be telescoping in time before our eyes.

Carlson Companies is my baby. It will be difficult to step away, but step away I must one day. The time is steadily approaching. The future will soon belong to others.

AFTERWORD

THE KIDS have an expression—what goes around comes around—which seems to me another way of saying there's nothing really new under the sun. The fact is, things in this life have a way of coming full circle, of repeating themselves—sometimes in surprising and exciting new ways.

That's the way I look at the subject of trading stamps. In Chapter Seventeen I talked about the potency of the trading-stamp concept in the 1990s, more than twenty years after the U.S. market saturation of the traditional paper-and-glue stamp; I mentioned the huge popularity of the airlines' frequent-flyer clubs and the lodging industry's frequent-guest plans, describing such programs as trading stamps in updated clothing. Well, before I sign off, I think it's appropriate to elaborate a bit on Carlson Companies' own updated "stamp" activity, which brings us, in a very real sense, all the way back to our beginnings. Stamps were where we started in 1938, and in 1994 the stamp concept is one of the most exciting and promising parts of our business. What our new, "electronic stamp" amounts to is a new twist on an old idea, incorporating technologies undreamed of when we started, but performing exactly the same fundamental role for our customers —helping them improve their business.

The idea had been buzzing around in my head since 1990. I watched the evolution of the supermarket business in the '70s and '80s, when trading stamps were abandoned in favor of discount pricing, and eventually began seeing striking parallels with the early '50s, when the big chains relied solely on a couple pennies' worth of difference on the same basic products to differentiate themselves from the competition. I also watched the growing enthusiasm for loyalty programs in select department stores and in the airline and hospitality industries, where, of course, we've long been a major player. I thought, Why not take the basic stamp idea, replace the paper and glue with digital technology, and give progressive, innovative grocers the means with which to stand their industry on its head once more?

In January 1993, after working on the idea for a couple of years, I formally presented it during our annual sales meeting. When I'd finished speaking, I added, "And the guy who's going to sell this program is sitting in the back row!"—surprising at least one person in the audience, my old pal Harry Greenough. What goes around comes around indeed! Harry, you'll remember, was the guy who played such an important part in Gold Bond Stamps' breakthrough with the supermarkets forty years ago. Though he was living in comfortable retirement in Florida, Greenough, who'd succeeded me as Gold Bond president when we diversified, was the obvious choice to make another run at the grocery industry.

Thankfully, Harry agreed to come back to work. He quickly went out and conducted his own "survey in the brush," taking a hard look at today's retail grocery environment, its problems, and its needs. He saw what I'd seen—widespread consolidation, store closings, Chapter XI filings, management upheaval, layoffs, and price disruption that signaled a broken industry. No one seemed able to generate a meaningful and long-lasting competitive edge. The few loyalty programs that existed were small and limited and played no significant role in the business.

We decided to go ahead with our own unique plan, which we named Gold Points Plus and which is designed for the leading grocery stores in fifty major U.S. markets. (This past April we also launched our Value First Discount Points program targeted for smaller North American markets.) Simply put, Gold Points Plus is an electronic loyalty-points program identical to stamps, except, as Harry says, "it's a hell of a lot better." It's better because participating consumers know where they stand every time they shop, and it's better because there are so many more ways to redeem their "stamps."

In the old days people stashed trading stamps in their pockets and purses, in kitchen cupboards and dining-room drawers, in the glove compartment of their cars. Now "savers" need only a magnetic card, and everything they have to know is kept up-to-date on retailers' computers. Now, too, consumers can use their points to buy weekly specials at the supermarket, can cash their points in for $10 certificates that may be spent on merchandise either at that market or any of the dozens of neighboring cosponsoring stores (what we used to call associate accounts), can redeem them for hundreds of popular premiums in our gift catalog, or can use them at participating hotels and restaurants, for major league sporting events, and even for frequent-flyer discounts.

Never before has a "stamp" program given consumers greater bang for their retail dollar. Never before has a "stamp" program given participating retailers such a powerful competitive tool to bring consumers into their stores and to keep them coming back. I can only try to tell you how thrilled I am about the potential of this program, which I believe is going to be one of *our* most successful business builders as well. I must say, as I celebrate my eightieth birthday and look back on where this company started and how far it's come, I'm pleased with the symmetry of the whole notion, too.

That dynamic little trading stamp. It's clearly an idea whose time has come. Again.

INDEX